Party Treats

Contents

Birthdays

CHEWY PEANUT BUTTER BROWNIES

Makes about 3 dozen brownies

¾ cup (1½ sticks) butter, melted
¾ cup creamy peanut butter
1¾ cups sugar
2 teaspoons vanilla
4 eggs, lightly beaten
1¼ cups all-purpose flour
½ teaspoon baking powder
¼ teaspoon salt
¼ cup unsweetened cocoa powder

1. Preheat oven to 350°F. Grease 13×9-inch baking pan.

2. Combine butter and peanut butter in large bowl; mix well. Stir in sugar and vanilla. Add eggs; beat until well blended. Stir in flour, baking powder and salt just until blended. Remove 1¾ cups batter to small bowl; stir cocoa into remaining batter.

3. Spread cocoa batter evenly in bottom of prepared pan. Top with remaining 1¾ cups of reserved batter. Bake 30 minutes or until edges begin to pull away from sides of pan. Cool completely in pan on wire rack; cut into bars.

FUNNY FACE PIZZAS
Makes 4 servings

1 package (10 ounces) refrigerated pizza dough
1 cup pizza sauce
1 cup (4 ounces) shredded mozzarella cheese
    Assorted toppings: pepperoni, black olive slices, green or red bell pepper slices and/or mushroom slices
⅓ cup shredded Cheddar cheese

1. Preheat oven to 425°F. Spray baking sheet with nonstick cooking spray; set aside.

2. Remove dough from package. *Do not unroll dough.* Slice dough into 4 equal pieces. Knead each piece of dough until ball forms. Pat or roll each ball into 4-inch disk. Place disks on prepared baking sheet.

3. Spread ¼ cup sauce on each disk. Sprinkle with mozzarella cheese. Decorate with toppings as desired to create faces. Sprinkle with Cheddar cheese to resemble hair.

4. Bake 10 minutes or until cheese is just melted and bottoms of pizzas are light brown.

LOLLIPOP GARDEN BOUQUET

Makes 12 servings

1 package (18¼ ounces) carrot cake mix, plus ingredients to prepare mix
1 container (16 ounces) white frosting
   Green food coloring
½ cup crushed chocolate wafer cookies
   Round hard sweet and sour candies
20 hard candy rings
   Green chewy fruit snack
6 to 10 lollipops

1. Prepare and bake cake mix according to package directions for one 8-inch round cake and one 9-inch round cake. Cool completely before frosting.

2. Blend frosting and food coloring in medium bowl until desired shade is reached. Place 8-inch cake layer on serving plate; spread top with frosting. Top with 9-inch cake layer; frost top and side of cake.

3. Sprinkle top of cake with cookie crumbs, leaving 1-inch border around edge of cake. Arrange round candies around edge of cake as shown in photo. Press candy rings into side of bottom cake layer.

4. Use scissors to cut fruit snack into 2½-inch leaf shapes. Press leaves onto lollipop sticks; arrange lollipops in center of cake.

Lollipop Garden Bouquet

ULTIMATE THE ORIGINAL RANCH®
CHEESE BURGERS

Makes 4 servings

1 packet (1 ounce) HIDDEN VALLEY® The Original Ranch® Salad Dressing
    & Seasoning Mix
1 pound ground beef
1 cup (4 ounces) shredded Cheddar cheese
4 large hamburger buns, toasted

Combine dressing mix with beef and cheese. Shape into 4 patties; cook thoroughly until no longer pink in center. Serve on toasted buns.

THE ORIGINAL RANCH® ROASTED POTATOES

Makes 4 to 6 servings

2 pounds small red potatoes, quartered
¼ cup vegetable oil
1 packet (1 ounce) HIDDEN VALLEY® The Original Ranch® Salad Dressing
    & Seasoning Mix

Place potatoes in a resealable plastic bag and add oil; seal bag. Toss to coat. Add salad dressing & seasoning mix and toss again until coated. Bake in an ungreased baking pan at 450°F for 35 minutes or until potatoes are brown and crisp.

PARTY MINTS

Makes 3 dozen mints

1 (14-ounce) can EAGLE BRAND® Sweetened Condensed Milk (NOT
   evaporated milk)
1 (32-ounce) package confectioners' sugar
½ teaspoon peppermint extract
   Assorted colored granulated sugar or crystals

1. In medium bowl, beat EAGLE BRAND® and half of confectioners' sugar until
blended. Gradually add remaining confectioners' sugar and peppermint extract,
beating until stiff.

2. Shape mixture into ½-inch balls. Roll in desired sugar; place on parchment
paper. Let stand 8 hours to set. Store covered at room temperature.

Prep Time: 30 minutes
Stand Time: 8 hours

You
may instead want to dip
uncoated mints in melted
bittersweet chocolate. Simply place
chocolate in a small microwavable
bowl and heat for 60 seconds
per ounce.

GIANT GIFT BOXES

Makes 12 servings

1 package (18¼ ounces) chocolate or vanilla cake mix, plus ingredients
  to prepare mix
1 container (16 ounces) white frosting
  Green and orange food coloring
  Yellow decorating icing
  Candy sprinkles
  Candles

1. Prepare and bake cake mix according to package directions for two 8- or 9-inch square cakes. Cool completely before frosting.

2. Blend half of frosting and green food coloring in medium bowl until desired shade is reached. Repeat with remaining frosting and orange food coloring.

3. Place one cake layer on serving plate; frost top and sides with green frosting. Pipe stripe of icing on each side to resemble ribbon. Let frosting set before adding second cake layer. Place second cake layer slightly off-center and rotated 45 degrees from bottom layer using photo as guide. Frost top and sides with orange frosting. Pipe stripe of icing on each side to resemble ribbon.

4. Pipe additional icing on top of cake for bow and streamers as shown in photo. Decorate cake with candy sprinkles and candles.

BACON-WRAPPED BBQ CHICKEN

Makes 4 servings

8 chicken tender strips, patted dry (about 1 pound)
½ teaspoon paprika or cumin (optional)
8 slices bacon
½ cup barbecue sauce

1. Preheat broiler. Line broiler pan with foil and set aside.

2. Sprinkle chicken strips with seasoning, if desired. Wrap each chicken strip with one slice of bacon in spiral; place on broiler pan.

3. Broil chicken 4 minutes; turn and broil 2 minutes more. Remove from oven and brush with ¼ cup barbecue sauce. Broil 2 minutes. Remove from oven, turn over chicken strips and baste with remaining barbecue sauce. Broil 2 minutes more. Serve immediately.

RICH & MEATY PIZZA CUP SNACKS

Makes 10 pizza cups

1 can (12 ounces) refrigerated biscuits (10 biscuits)
1½ cups RAGÚ® Rich & Meaty Meat Sauce
½ cup shredded mozzarella cheese (about 2 ounces)

1. Preheat oven to 375°F. In 12-cup muffin pan, evenly press each biscuit in bottom and up sides of each cup; chill until ready to fill.

2. Evenly spoon Meat Sauce into prepared muffin cups. Bake 15 minutes. Evenly sprinkle tops with cheese and bake an additional 5 minutes or until cheese is melted and biscuits are golden. Let stand 5 minutes before serving. Gently remove pizza cups from muffin pan and serve.

Prep Time: 10 minutes
Cook Time: 20 minutes

CHERRY CHOCOLATE FROSTY

Makes 1 (¾-cup) serving

1 container (6 ounces) chocolate yogurt
½ cup frozen dark sweet cherries
⅛ to ¼ teaspoon almond extract

1. Place all ingredients in blender container. Cover; process 15 to 30 seconds until smooth, using on/off pulsing action to break up chunks.

2. Pour into glass and serve.

ROCKIN' RASPBERRY REFRESHERS

Makes 2 servings

½ cup fresh or thawed frozen unsweetened raspberries
¼ cup frozen pink lemonade concentrate
2 cups club soda, chilled

1. Place raspberries and lemonade concentrate in blender. Cover; blend on HIGH speed until smooth. Add ½ cup club soda to blender; cover and blend until mixed.

2. Pour remaining 1½ cups club soda into small pitcher. Add raspberry mixture; stir. Pour into glasses and serve immediately.

Valentine's Day

ICE CREAM SANDWICH HEARTS

Makes 8 sandwiches

2 packages (18 ounces each) refrigerated peanut butter cookie dough
2 tablespoons finely chopped peanuts
2 cups vanilla or chocolate ice cream, softened
 Chocolate sauce or melted chocolate

1. Preheat oven to 350°F. Grease 15×10-inch jelly-roll pan. Let dough stand at room temperature about 15 minutes.

2. Press cookie dough evenly into prepared pan. Sprinkle with peanuts, pressing nuts in lightly.

3. Bake 22 to 25 minutes or until set and golden brown. Cool completely in pan on wire rack.

4. Use 3-inch heart-shaped cookie cutter to cut out 16 hearts. (Reserve scraps for snacking or discard.) Spoon ¼ cup ice cream onto 8 hearts; top with remaining hearts. Press each sandwich gently to spread ice cream to edges, scraping any excess from edges. To serve, place sandwiches on plates and drizzle with chocolate sauce.

Make-Ahead Time: up to 2 days
Final Prep Time: 10 minutes

BLACK & WHITE HEARTS

Makes about 3½ dozen cookies

    1 cup (2 sticks) butter, softened
    ¾ cup sugar
    1 package (3 ounces) cream cheese, softened
    1 egg
1½ teaspoons vanilla
    3 cups all-purpose flour
    1 cup semisweet chocolate chips
    2 tablespoons shortening

1. Beat butter, sugar, cream cheese, egg and vanilla in large bowl with electric mixer at medium speed, scraping bowl often, until light and fluffy. Add flour; beat until well blended. Divide dough in half; wrap each half in plastic wrap. Refrigerate 2 hours or until firm.

2. Preheat oven to 375°F. Roll dough to ⅛-inch thickness on lightly floured surface. Cut dough with lightly floured 2-inch heart-shaped cookie cutter. Place cutouts 1 inch apart on ungreased cookie sheets. Bake 7 to 10 minutes or until edges are very lightly browned. Remove immediately to wire racks; cool completely.

3. Melt chocolate chips and shortening in small saucepan over low heat 4 to 6 minutes or until melted. Dip half of each heart into melted chocolate. Refrigerate on cookie sheets or trays lined with waxed paper until chocolate is set. Store covered in refrigerator.

Black & White Hearts

CHERRY-FILLED HEARTS

Makes 10 servings

½ **package (17¼ ounces) frozen puff pastry sheets (1 sheet), thawed**
1 **egg yolk**
1 **teaspoon water**
1 **can (21 ounces) cherry pie filling**
¼ **teaspoon almond extract**
1 **cup hot fudge topping, heated, divided**
2½ **cups thawed frozen nondairy whipped topping**

1. Preheat oven to 400°F.

2. Unfold puff pastry sheet on lightly floured surface. Use 3-inch heart-shaped cookie cutter to cut out 10 hearts from pastry. Place on ungreased baking sheet.

3. Combine egg yolk and water in small bowl; beat lightly with fork until well blended. Brush evenly onto pastry cutouts, covering completely. Bake 10 to 12 minutes or until golden brown. Cool on wire rack.

4. Meanwhile, combine pie filling and extract in medium saucepan. Cook over low heat, stirring occasionally, until heated through.

5. Spoon about 1 tablespoon fudge topping onto each of 10 dessert plates. Carefully split each heart horizontally in half. Place bottom halves of hearts on plates; top evenly with pie filling mixture and whipped topping. Replace top halves of hearts. Drizzle evenly with remaining fudge topping.

SAVORY SWEETIE PIES

Makes 15 appetizer servings

2 tablespoons all-purpose flour
1 teaspoon rubbed sage
¼ teaspoon salt
¼ teaspoon black pepper
½ pound boneless skinless chicken breasts, chopped
2 tablespoons butter or margarine
1 cup chicken broth
1 cup thawed frozen mixed vegetables
1 package (15 ounces) refrigerated pie crusts
1 egg yolk
1 teaspoon water

1. Preheat oven to 400°F. Lightly grease baking sheets.

2. Combine flour, sage, salt and pepper in medium bowl. Add chicken; toss to coat.

3. Melt butter in large skillet over medium heat. Add chicken and any remaining flour mixture; cook, stirring frequently, 5 minutes or until chicken is no longer pink in center. Stir in broth and vegetables. Reduce heat to low; simmer 5 to 8 minutes or until mixture is heated through.

4. Roll out 1 pie crust to 14-inch diameter on floured surface. Cut out about 15 heart shapes using 3-inch heart-shaped cookie cutter. Repeat with second pie crust, rerolling pastry scraps if necessary, to get a total of 30 hearts. Place half of the hearts on prepared baking sheets; top each with heaping tablespoonful chicken mixture. Cover with remaining hearts; press edges together with fork to seal.

5. Combine egg yolk and water in small bowl; mix until well blended. Brush onto hearts.

6. Bake 15 to 20 minutes or until golden brown.

SWEETEST HEART CAKE

Makes 12 to 16 servings

1 (8-inch) round cake, any flavor
1 (8-inch) square cake, any flavor
1 container (16 ounces) vanilla frosting, tinted pink with
    red food coloring
1½ cups flaked coconut, tinted pink to match frosting*
2 large red gumdrops
    Granulated sugar
1 large white gumdrop
    Red chewy fruit snack

To tint coconut, combine small amount of food coloring (paste or liquid) with 1 teaspoon water in large bowl. Add coconut and stir until evenly coated. Add more coloring, if needed.

1. Cut round cake in half to make two semi-circles.

2. Position square cake and semi-circles on large serving plate using photo as guide, connecting with some frosting. Frost entire cake with remaining frosting. Sprinkle evenly with coconut.

3. Flatten 1 red gumdrop with rolling pin on lightly sugared surface to make small heart. Cut out heart shape with small cookie cutter. Repeat with remaining red gumdrop and white gumdrop. Place 3 gumdrop hearts on cake, overlapping slightly as shown in photo.

4. Cut chewy fruit snack into ½-inch strips. Tie strips into loose bow and place on cake.

Sweetest Heart Cake

CHOCOLATE AND PEANUT BUTTER HEARTS

Makes 4 dozen cookies

Chocolate Cookie Dough (page 28)
 1 cup sugar
 ½ cup creamy peanut butter
 ½ cup shortening
 1 egg
 3 tablespoons milk
 1 teaspoon vanilla
 2 cups all-purpose flour
 1 teaspoon baking powder
 ¼ teaspoon salt

1. Prepare and chill Chocolate Cookie Dough.

2. Beat sugar, peanut butter and shortening until fluffy. Add egg, milk and vanilla; mix well. Combine flour, baking powder and salt. Beat flour mixture into peanut butter mixture until well blended. Shape dough into disc. Wrap in plastic wrap; refrigerate 1 to 2 hours or until firm.

3. Preheat oven to 350°F. Grease cookie sheets. Roll out peanut butter dough on floured waxed paper to ⅛-inch thickness. Cut dough using 3-inch heart-shaped cookie cutters or smaller cookie cutters, if desired. Place cutouts on prepared cookie sheets. Repeat with chocolate dough.

4. Use smaller heart-shaped cookie cutters to cut small heart shapes from centers of large heart cutouts. Place small peanut butter hearts into large chocolate hearts; place small chocolate hearts into large peanut butter hearts. Press together lightly.

5. Bake 12 to 14 minutes or until edges are lightly browned. Remove to wire racks; cool completely.

continued on page 28

Chocolate and Peanut Butter Hearts

Chocolate and Peanut Butter Hearts, continued

CHOCOLATE COOKIE DOUGH

    1 cup (2 sticks) butter, softened
    1 cup sugar
    1 egg
    1 teaspoon vanilla
    2 ounces semisweet chocolate, melted
 2¼ cups all-purpose flour
    1 teaspoon baking powder
  ¼ teaspoon salt

1. Beat butter and sugar in large bowl with electric mixer at high speed until fluffy. Beat in egg and vanilla. Add melted chocolate; mix well.

2. Add flour, baking powder and salt; mix well. Cover; refrigerate about 2 hours or until firm.

SIMPLE MOLDED CANDY

Makes about 2 dozen candies

 12 ounces confectionery coating
    Food coloring
    Valentine shaped molds

1. Melt confectionery coating in bowl over hot, not boiling water, stirring constantly. Add food coloring, a few drops at a time, until desired shade is reached.

2. Spoon into molds. Tap molds on countertop to remove bubbles. Refrigerate until firm. Bring to room temperature before unmolding to avoid cracking molds.

VARIATION: To make two-tone candies, choose molds with sections to allow for layering. Melt coating as directed. Spoon first layer of coating into molds; tap molds on countertop to remove bubbles. Refrigerate until firm. Spoon second layer into molds. Proceed as directed above.

LACY HEARTS CAKE

Makes 12 to 16 servings

Creamy White Frosting (recipe follows)
2 (8-inch) round cake layers
Base Frosting (recipe follows)
Red cinnamon candies
Red sugar

SUPPLIES

1 (10-inch) cake plate or round cake board, covered
Paper doily

1. Prepare Creamy White Frosting. If cake tops are rounded, trim horizontally with long serrated knife. Place one cake layer on cake plate. Spread about ½ cup Creamy White Frosting on cake and top with second cake layer.

2. Prepare Base Frosting; frost entire cake to seal in crumbs. Let stand until set. Frost again with remaining Creamy White Frosting.

3. Cut out heart shape from doily. For overlapping heart decoration, place doily heart on cake top about ½ inch from left edge of cake. Place candies around left edge of pattern and about 1½ inches up right side from point, pressing gently into frosting.

4. Carefully lift off doily heart. Reposition doily heart on cake top, fitting left edge of pattern into space of first heart and about ½ inch from right edge of cake. (Be sure bottom points of hearts align.) Place candies around pattern to outline heart.

5. Sprinkle sugar over doily heart so sugar goes through holes, being careful to sprinkle only over doily. Brush sugar through holes in doily with fingertip. Lift off doily heart, being careful to brush any sugar that clings to doily heart inside outlined heart.

6. Position left half of doily heart over left outlined heart and sprinkle with sugar. Lift off doily heart. Use toothpick to remove any sugar outside outlined hearts.

7. Place single row of candies around bottom edge of cake, pressing gently into frosting.

CREAMY WHITE FROSTING

Makes enough to frost 2 (8-inch) round cake layers

½ cup shortening
6 cups sifted powdered sugar, divided
3 tablespoons milk
2 teaspoons clear vanilla
   Additional milk*

For thinner frosting, use more milk and for thicker frosting use less milk.

1. Beat shortening in large bowl with electric mixer at medium speed until fluffy.

2. Gradually beat in 3 cups sugar until well blended and smooth. Carefully beat in 3 tablespoons milk and vanilla.

3. Gradually beat in remaining 3 cups sugar, adding more milk, 1 teaspoon at a time, as needed for good spreading consistency.

BASE FROSTING

Makes about 2 cups

3 cups powdered sugar, sifted
½ cup shortening
¼ cup milk
½ teaspoon vanilla
   Additional milk

1. Beat sugar, shortening, ¼ cup milk and vanilla with electric mixer on medium speed in large bowl until smooth.

2. Add more milk, 1 teaspoon at a time, until frosting is thin consistency.

STRAWBERRY HEARTS

Makes about 2 dozen hearts

1 package (18 ounces) refrigerated sugar cookie dough
2 packages (8 ounces each) cream cheese, softened
⅔ cup powdered sugar
1 teaspoon vanilla
2 cups sliced fresh strawberries

1. Remove dough from wrapper. Roll out dough; cut out hearts with 2-inch heart-shaped cookie cutter and bake as directed on package.

2. Combine cream cheese, powdered sugar and vanilla; mix well.

3. Spread evenly onto cooled hearts; top evenly with strawberries.

SWEETHEART PIZZETTES

Makes 16 appetizer servings

2 cups sour cream
½ package (1.4 ounces) dry vegetable soup mix (about ⅓ cup)
1 can (10 ounces) refrigerated pizza dough
3 tablespoons grated Parmesan cheese (optional)
½ cup chopped plum tomatoes

1. Combine sour cream and soup mix in small bowl; stir until well blended. Cover; refrigerate 2 to 3 hours or overnight.

2. Preheat oven to 425°F. Grease baking sheets; set aside.

3. Unroll pizza dough on floured surface; roll out to 15×13-inch rectangle. Using 2-inch heart-shaped cookie cutter, cut out 16 hearts. Cut out smaller hearts from any remaining scraps of dough, if desired. Place on prepared baking sheets; sprinkle evenly with Parmesan cheese. Bake 8 to 10 minutes or until golden brown. Remove to wire racks to cool slightly.

4. To serve, spread sour cream mixture evenly onto hearts and top evenly with tomatoes.

Strawberry Hearts, Sweetheart Pizzettes and
Savory Sweetie Pies (page 25)

CHOCOLATE-DIPPED STRAWBERRIES

Makes 12 strawberries

> 2 cups (11½ ounces) milk chocolate chips
> 1 tablespoon shortening
> 12 large strawberries with stems, rinsed and dried

1. Line baking sheet with waxed paper; set aside.

2. Melt chips with shortening in top of double boiler over hot, not boiling, water, stirring constantly.

3. Dip about half of each strawberry in chocolate. Remove excess chocolate by scraping bottom of strawberry across rim of pan. Place strawberries on prepared baking sheet. Let stand until set.

4. Store in refrigerator in airtight container between layers of waxed paper.

VARIATION: Melt 8 ounces white chocolate or pastel confectionery coating. Dip bottoms of dipped strawberries, leaving a portion of the milk chocolate coating showing.

TIP: Stir chopped dried fruits, raisins or nuts into any remaining chocolate; drop by tablespoonfuls onto a baking sheet lined with waxed paper.

VALENTINE SMOOTHIES

Makes 2 servings

1 cup vanilla yogurt
1 ripe banana, sliced
2 tablespoons strawberry jam
1 tablespoon honey or granulated sugar
3 or 4 drops red food coloring

1. Combine all ingredients in blender container; cover. Blend at high 20 seconds or until foamy.

2. Pour into 2 glasses and serve immediately. Garnish as desired.

Prep and Cook Time: 3 minutes

Bees have been producing honey for millions of years. A worker bee will toil for an entire lifetime to make $\frac{1}{12}$ teaspoon of honey (about 3 drops).

CUPID CAKES

Makes 12 servings

1 package (10 ounces) frozen strawberries, thawed and coarsely chopped
1 tablespoon powdered sugar
½ cup whipping cream, whipped
2 frozen all-butter pound cakes (10¾ ounces each), thawed
½ cup strawberry preserves

1. Drain strawberries; reserve 1 tablespoon juice. Gently combine strawberries, reserved juice and powdered sugar with whipped cream; set aside.

2. Cut each cake into 12 slices. Spread half of slices with about 1½ teaspoons preserves. Top with remaining slices to make sandwiches. Press each sandwich gently to spread preserves to edges, scraping any excess from edges. Place onto serving plates; top with whipped cream mixture.

Prep and Cook Time: 15 minutes

Halloween

FEET OF MEAT

Makes 8 to 10 servings

2½ pounds ground beef
1 clove garlic, minced
½ cup bread crumbs or oatmeal
½ cup milk or water
1 egg
1 envelope (1 ounce) dry onion soup mix
8 Brazil nuts or almonds
2 tablespoons barbecue sauce or ketchup

1. Preheat oven to 350°F. Combine ground beef, garlic, bread crumbs, milk, egg and onion soup mix in large bowl; stir until well blended. Reserve 1 cup meat mixture.

2. Divide remaining meat mixture in half; shape each half into 7×4-inch oval. Place ovals on rimmed baking sheet. Divide reserved 1 cup meat mixture into 8 balls; place 4 balls at end of each oval for toes. Press 1 nut into each toe for toenails. Brush meat loaves with barbecue sauce; bake 1½ hours until meat thermometer registers 160°F.

TIP: When shaping feet, form "ankles" that have been "cut off" and fill them with dripping ketchup before serving for an especially gruesome effect!

MERINGUE BONE COOKIES

Makes 2 dozen cookies

1½ **cups sugar**
  Pinch of salt
 5 egg whites at room temperature
  Pinch of cream of tartar
 1 teaspoon almond, vanilla, orange or lemon extract

1. Preheat oven to 220°F. Line 2 cookie sheets with parchment paper. Prepare pastry bag with round #10 tip (about ⅜-inch diameter).

2. Combine sugar and salt in small bowl. Beat egg whites and cream of tartar in small bowl with electric mixer at low speed until soft peaks form. Gradually add sugar mixture, beating constantly. Beat until stiff peaks form and meringue is shiny and smooth. Add extract; beat just until blended.

3. Fill pastry bag with meringue. Pipe log 3 to 4 inches long. Pipe 2 balls on both ends of each log. Smooth any peaks with wet finger. Repeat with remaining meringue.

4. Bake 30 minutes; turn off heat. Leave cookies in oven overnight; do not open oven door.

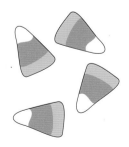

SMASHED THUMBSTICKS WITH OILY DIPPING SAUCE

Makes 12 appetizers

THUMBSTICKS

> 1 can (11 ounces) refrigerated breadstick dough
> 12 sun-dried tomatoes, cut in half crosswise or 12 jumbo pitted ripe
>   olives, halved lengthwise
> 2 tablespoons olive oil
>   Dried basil or dill

DIPPING SAUCE

> ½ cup olive oil
> 2 tablespoons balsamic vinegar
> 1 teaspoon dried basil
> ½ teaspoon salt
> ¼ teaspoon black pepper

1. Preheat oven to 375°F. Unroll breadstick dough; separate each strip and cut in half crosswise. Place on 2 ungreased baking sheets. Place tomato half about ⅛ inch from top of each strip and press down firmly; shape ends to round out tip of thumb.

2. Gently press down on dough with knife in 2 places to resemble knuckles. Brush breadsticks with 2 tablespoons olive oil; sprinkle with basil. Bake 10 minutes or until light golden brown.

3. Meanwhile, combine dipping sauce ingredients in 1-pint jar; cover and shake until well blended. Serve with Smashed Thumbsticks.

BLOODSHOT EYEBALLS

Makes about 2½ dozen cookies

2¾ cups all-purpose flour
1 teaspoon baking soda
½ teaspoon salt
1 cup (2 sticks) butter, softened
¾ cup granulated sugar
¾ cup packed light brown sugar
2 eggs
1 teaspoon vanilla
1 container (16 ounces) white frosting
Green or blue gummy candy rings
1 tube (0.6 ounce) black decorating gel
1 tube (0.6 ounce) red decorating gel

1. Combine flour, baking soda and salt in small bowl. Beat together butter and sugars in large bowl with electric mixer on medium speed until light and fluffy. Beat in eggs, one at a time. Beat in vanilla. Add flour mixture gradually, mixing well. Divide dough into two oval discs. Wrap in plastic wrap and chill at least 30 minutes.

2. Preheat oven to 375°F. Roll out dough on lightly floured surface to ⅛-inch thickness. Draw oval "eye" shape (about 4×2 inches) on piece of cardboard. Cut out shape and use as stencil for cutting cookie dough. Place cutouts 2 inches apart on ungreased cookie sheets. Bake 9 to 11 minutes or until golden brown. Transfer to wire racks; cool completely.

3. Spread frosting evenly over cooled cookies. Use candy rings to form an "iris" on each cookie. Fill in pupils and make eyelashes with black decorating gel. Decorate cookies with red decorating gel for bloodshot effect.

COFFIN COOKIES

Makes about 2 dozen sandwich cookies

1 package (18 ounces) refrigerated chocolate cookie dough*
Marshmallow Filling (recipe follows)
Colored sprinkles and sugars
Prepared white icing
Halloween decors

If refrigerated chocolate cookie dough is unavailable, add ¼ cup unsweetened cocoa powder to refrigerated sugar cookie dough. Beat in large bowl until well blended.

1. Draw and cut out pattern for coffin on cardboard using photo as guide. Preheat oven to 350°F. Remove dough from wrapper; divide dough in half. Reserve 1 half; wrap remaining half in plastic wrap and refrigerate.

2. Roll reserved dough on lightly floured surface to ⅛-inch thickness. Sprinkle with flour to minimize sticking, if necessary. Place pattern on cookie dough; cut dough around pattern with sharp knife. Repeat with remaining dough and scraps. Place cutouts 2 inches apart on ungreased cookie sheets.

3. Bake about 6 minutes or just until firm but not browned. Cool on cookie sheets 2 minutes. Remove to wire racks; cool completely.

4. Prepare Marshmallow Filling. Spread half of cookies with 2 teaspoons filling; top with remaining cookies. Dip cookie sandwich edges in sprinkles. Decorate with icing and decors as desired.

MARSHMALLOW FILLING

Makes 1¾ cups

1 cup prepared vanilla frosting
¾ cup marshmallow creme

Mix frosting and marshmallow creme in small bowl until well blended.

SLOPPY GOBLINS

Makes 8 servings

1 pound ground beef
1 cup chopped onion
5 hot dogs, cut into ½-inch pieces
½ cup ketchup
¼ cup chopped dill pickle
¼ cup honey
¼ cup tomato paste
¼ cup prepared mustard
2 teaspoons cider vinegar
1 teaspoon Worcestershire sauce
8 hamburger buns
   Green and black olives
   Banana pepper slices
   Baby carrots

1. Cook beef and onion in large skillet 6 to 8 minutes over medium heat, stirring to break up meat. Drain fat. Stir in remaining ingredients except buns, olives, pepper slices and carrots. Cook, covered, 5 minutes or until heated through.

2. Spoon meat mixture onto bottoms of buns; cover with tops of buns. Serve with olives, pepper slices and carrots. Each person can create their own goblin face. Refrigerate any leftovers.

Sloppy Goblin

SNAIL CAKE

Makes 1 cake

1 package (18¼ ounces) yellow cake mix, plus ingredients to
    prepare mix
⅓ cup seedless red raspberry preserves
2 containers (12 ounces each) whipped cream cheese frosting
    Assorted food coloring: blue, green, yellow and red
    Red string licorice
    Candy-coated chocolate peanuts
10 gingersnaps, crushed
    Chocolate pebbles
    Rock candy

1. Prepare and bake cake mix in two 9-inch cake pans according to package directions. Cool cakes in pans on wire rack 10 minutes. Remove cakes to wire rack; cool completely.

2. Spread jam on 1 cake layer; top with second layer. Looking down on cake, measure 6 inches from top; using serrated knife, cut across cake (diagram A). Stand larger cake section (snail shell) upright on long serving platter. To keep serving platter neat, place long strips of waxed paper around perimeter of platter and slightly under cake. Tint 1 container frosting teal (blue with hint of green) and frost snail shell. Add green food coloring to remaining teal frosting and place in pastry bag fitted with #6 tip. Pipe swirl pattern on sides of shell.

3. Place remaining half-circle cake section on counter. Cut out snail's tail and head section. There will be scraps when forming head. Place half of remaining frosting in medium bowl; tint peach using yellow and red coloring. Attach head and tail to shell; frost with peach-colored frosting (diagram B).

4. Place piece of licorice string on face to resemble smiling mouth and 2 pieces for antennae. Use candy-coated chocolate peanuts for eyes. Remove waxed paper. To decorate serving platter, spread thin layer of frosting on platter; sprinkle with ground cookies to resemble sand. Scatter with chocolate pebbles and rock candy.

A
SNAIL SHELL
6"
❶
❷
TAIL
❸
SCRAP
SCRAP
HEAD

B
❸ ❶ ❷

SPIDER CAKES

Makes 18 to 20 cupcakes

18 to 20 chocolate cupcakes
1 box (4-serving size) white chocolate pudding mix, prepared according to package directions and tinted green with food coloring
1 container (16 ounces) fudge frosting
Halloween cupcake liners
Black licorice, cut in half for spider legs
Red cinnamon candies for eyes
2 black licorice strings, cut into ¼-inch pieces for eyelashes (optional)

1. Poke small hole in bottom of each cupcake with toothpick. Snip off corner of resealable food storage bag with scissors, making hole just large enough for small, round piping tip to fit through. Place tip into opening. Spoon green pudding into bag.

2. Insert piping tip into bottom of cupcake. Pipe some pudding gently and slowly into each cake.

3. Frost tops and sides of cupcakes with frosting. Place each cupcake in slightly flattened cupcake liner.

4. Place 4 pieces of licorice on each side of cupcake to form legs. Press in cinnamon candies for eyes. Press licorice strings above cinnamon candies to create eyelashes, if desired. Serve immediately.

Create an even better tasting fudge frosting by adding ½ teaspoon almond or mint extract.

Spider Cakes

CREEPY COBWEBS

Makes 10 to 12 servings

4 to 5 cups vegetable oil
1 cup pancake mix
¾ cup plus 2 tablespoons milk
1 egg, beaten
½ cup powdered sugar
1 teaspoon ground cinnamon
½ teaspoon chili powder
   Dipping Sauce (recipe follows)

1. Pour 1 inch of oil into heavy, deep 10-inch skillet. Heat oil to 350°F.

2. Combine pancake mix, milk, egg and 1 tablespoon oil in medium bowl. Do not overmix. Put 2 tablespoons batter into funnel or squeeze bottle; swirl into hot oil to form cobwebs. Fry over medium-high heat 1 to 2 minutes or until bubbles form. Using tongs and slotted spatula, gently turn and fry 1 minute or until brown. Drain on cookie sheet lined with paper towels.

3. Repeat with remaining batter. If necessary, add more oil to maintain 1-inch depth, but heat oil to 350°F again before frying more batter.

4. Meanwhile, mix powdered sugar, cinnamon and chili powder in small bowl. Sprinkle over cobwebs. Place cobwebs on serving platter with Dipping Sauce.

DIPPING SAUCE

Makes 1 cup

1 cup maple syrup
1 jalapeño pepper,* cored, seeded and minced

*Jalapeño peppers can sting and irritate the skin, so wear rubber gloves when handling peppers and do not touch your eyes.

Combine syrup and jalapeño in small saucepan. Simmer 5 minutes or until syrup is hot. Pour into heat-proof bowl.

LIME CHILLERS WITH BLOOD DRIPPINGS

Makes 10 servings

¼ cup honey or corn syrup
12 drops red food coloring
4 cups chilled pineapple juice
6 ounces frozen limeade concentrate
3 cups chilled ginger ale

1. Combine honey and food coloring in shallow pan; mix until well blended. Dip rims of 10 wine goblets into mixture one at a time, coating rims. Turn upright and let stand to allow mixture to drip down sides, resembling blood. Place paper towel around base of goblets to catch drips.

2. Combine pineapple juice and limeade in punch bowl. Stir until limeade dissolves; stir in ginger ale. Fill each wine goblet with lime chiller.

TOASTED CHEESE JACK-O'-LANTERNS

Makes 4 servings

3 tablespoons butter or margarine, softened
8 slices bread
4 slices Monterey Jack cheese
4 slices sharp Cheddar cheese

1. Preheat oven to 350°F. Spread butter on one side of each bread slice. Place bread, buttered side down, on ungreased cookie sheet.

2. Cut out shapes from 4 bread slices using paring knife to make jack-o'-lantern faces. Layer 1 slice Monterey Jack and 1 slice Cheddar on remaining 4 bread slices.

3. Bake 10 to 12 minutes or until cheese is melted. Remove from oven; place jack-o'-lantern bread slice on sandwiches. Serve immediately.

Halloween

SKELETON COOKIES

Makes about 2 dozen cookies

30 to 40 drops black food coloring
1 package (18 ounces) refrigerated sugar cookie dough
Skeleton or gingerbread man cookie cutters
1 tube white frosting

1. Knead food coloring into cookie dough on lightly floured surface.* Wrap in plastic wrap and refrigerate 2 hours or until very firm.

2. Preheat oven to 350°F. Roll out dough on floured waxed paper to ⅛-inch thickness. Cut dough with cookie cutters. Bake 9 to 13 minutes or until edges are firm (centers will be somewhat soft). Cool 1 minute on cookie sheet; remove and cool completely on wire rack.

3. Draw skeleton figures on cookies with frosting as shown in photo.

Cookies will appear a shade or two lighter after baking, so, while kneading in the black food coloring, add a few more drops of coloring after the desired shade has been reached.

NOTE: The yield of this recipe is an approximation only and depends on the size of your cookie cutters and the thickness of the cookie dough.

Skeleton Cookies

Christmas

SNOWBALL BITES

Makes about 2½ dozen cookies

1 package (18 ounces) refrigerated sugar cookie dough
¾ cup all-purpose flour
2 tablespoons honey or maple syrup
1 cup chopped walnuts or pecans
   Powdered sugar

1. Let dough stand at room temperature about 15 minutes.

2. Beat dough, flour and honey in large bowl with electric mixer on medium speed until well blended. Stir in walnuts. Shape dough into disk; wrap tightly in plastic wrap. Refrigerate dough at least 2 hours or up to 2 days.

3. Preheat oven to 350°F. Place powdered sugar in small bowl; set aside. Shape dough into ¾-inch balls; place 1½ inches apart on ungreased cookie sheets.

4. Bake 10 to 12 minutes or until bottoms are browned. Roll warm cookies in powdered sugar. Cool completely on wire racks. Just before serving, roll cookies in additional powdered sugar, if desired.

CHOCOLATE ALMOND CHERRY MIX

Makes 6 cups

2 cups toasted almonds*
2 cups red and green candy coated chocolate pieces
2 cups dried cherries

To toast almonds, spread in a shallow baking pan. Bake in preheated 350°F oven 5 to 10 minutes or until golden brown, stirring frequently.

1. Combine all ingredients in large mixing bowl with wooden spoon.

2. To give as gifts or party favors, decorate individual resealable food storage bags. Spoon mix evenly into bags.

FESTIVE POPCORN TREATS

Makes 6 servings

6 cups popped popcorn
½ cup sugar
½ cup light corn syrup
¼ cup peanut butter
   Green food coloring
¼ cup red cinnamon candies

1. Line baking sheet with waxed paper.

2. Pour popcorn into large bowl. Combine sugar and corn syrup in medium saucepan. Bring to a boil over medium heat, stirring constantly; boil 1 minute. Remove from heat. Add peanut butter and green food coloring; stir until peanut butter is completely melted. Pour over popcorn; stir to coat well.

3. Lightly butter hands and shape popcorn mixture into cone shapes for trees. While trees are still warm, press red cinnamon candies into trees. Place on prepared baking sheet; let stand until firm, about 30 minutes.

HOLIDAY CANDY CANE TWISTS

Makes 8 servings

⅓ cup sugar
1 tablespoon ground cinnamon
1 can (11 ounces) refrigerated breadstick dough
3 tablespoons butter or margarine, melted
   Red decorating icing (optional)

1. Preheat oven to 350°F. Spray baking sheet with nonstick cooking spray.

2. Combine sugar and cinnamon in small bowl; mix well.

3. Separate dough; roll and stretch each piece of dough into 16-inch rope. Fold rope in half; twist ends together and form into candy cane shape on prepared baking sheet.

4. Brush candy canes with butter; sprinkle with cinnamon-sugar.

5. Bake 12 to 15 minutes or until golden brown. Serve warm, either plain or decorated with red icing as shown in photo.

CHRISTMAS TREE ROLLS: Make cinnamon-sugar with green colored sugar instead of granulated sugar. Stretch dough into 16-inch ropes as directed. Cut off ½ inch from 1 end of each rope for tree trunk. Shape ropes into tree shapes on prepared baking sheet; add trunks. Brush with butter and sprinkle with green cinnamon-sugar. Bake as directed. Decorate with red cinnamon candies.

Holiday Candy Cane Twists

KITTENS AND MITTENS

Makes about 2 dozen cookies

Chocolate Cookie Dough (page 28)
Cookie Glaze (page 75)
Assorted food colorings
Assorted candies

1. Preheat oven to 325°F. Grease cookie sheets.

2. Roll out dough on floured surface to ⅛-inch thickness. Cut out kitten and mitten cookie shapes, using photo as guide. Place cookies on prepared cookie sheets. Make holes in tops of cookies with plastic straw, about ½ inch from top edges.

3. Bake 8 to 10 minutes until edges begin to brown. Remove to wire racks; cool completely. If necessary, push straw through warm cookies to remake holes.

4. Place cookies on racks on waxed paper-lined baking sheets. Spoon Cookie Glaze into several small bowls. Tint as desired with food colorings. Spoon glaze over cookies. Place some of remaining glaze in plastic bag. Cut tiny tip from corner of bag. Use to pipe decorations. Decorate with candies. Let stand until glaze has set.

5. Thread yarn or ribbon through holes to make ornaments.

Unbaked cookie dough can be refrigerated for up to one week or frozen for up to six weeks. Rolls of dough should be sealed tightly in plastic wrap; other doughs should be stored in airtight containers.

FLUTED KISSES® CUPS WITH PEANUT BUTTER FILLING

Makes about 2 dozen pieces

72 HERSHEY.'S KISSES® Brand Milk Chocolates, divided
  1 cup REESE'S® Creamy Peanut Butter
  1 cup powdered sugar
  1 tablespoon butter or margarine, softened

1. Line small baking cups (1¾ inches in diameter) with small paper bake cups. Remove wrappers from chocolates.

2. Place 48 chocolates in small microwave-safe bowl. Microwave at HIGH (100%) 1 minute or until chocolate is melted and smooth when stirred. Using small brush, coat inside of paper cups with melted chocolate.

3. Refrigerate 20 minutes; reapply melted chocolate to any thin spots. Refrigerate until firm, preferably overnight. Gently peel paper from chocolate cups.

4. Beat peanut butter, powdered sugar and butter with electric mixer on medium speed in small bowl until smooth. Spoon into chocolate cups. Before serving, top each cup with a chocolate piece. Cover; store cups in refrigerator.

QUICK CANDY ORNAMENTS

Makes 4 to 6 ornaments

INGREDIENTS

1 package (7.5 ounces) hard candies, assorted colors
4 to 6 (2- or 3-inch) ovenproof open-topped cookie cutters

SUPPLIES

Clear nylon thread

1. Unwrap candies. Separate into colors; place each color in separate heavy resealable food storage bag. Crush candies with rolling pin.

2. Preheat oven to 400°F. Line baking sheet with foil; spray with nonstick cooking spray. Cut 6 pieces of foil, each about 8 inches square; fold each piece in half.

3. Place 1 cookie cutter in center of each piece of doubled foil; bring sides of foil up around cookie cutter, keeping foil in center as flat as possible. Press foil tightly to all sides of cutters. Place on prepared baking sheet, open tops facing up.

4. Spoon crushed candies into cookie cutters to depth of about ½ inch. Bake 8 to 10 minutes or until candy is melted. Meanwhile, cut thread into 6 (8-inch) lengths; bring ends of thread together and tie in knots. Remove ornaments from oven. While candy is warm, soft and still in cutter, place knotted end of thread near top of each shape for hanging; press into ornament with handle of wooden spoon. Cool completely.

5. Peel foil off ornaments. Gently bend cutters to loosen ornaments. Break or scrape off ragged edges of ornaments with small knife.

Quick Candy Ornaments and
Have-A-Heart Bear Garland (page 74)

HAVE-A-HEART BEAR GARLAND

Makes about 2 dozen cookies

1 recipe Butter Cookie dough (recipe follows)
1 recipe Cookie Glaze (recipe follows)
3 tablespoons unsweetened cocoa powder
  Powdered sugar
  Yellow food coloring (optional)
  Assorted candies

SUPPLIES

1 (3½- to 4-inch) bear-shaped cookie cutter
  Plastic drinking straw
1 (½-inch) heart-shaped cookie cutter
  Pastry bags and small writing tip
  Ribbon

1. Preheat oven to 350°F. Roll out dough to ¼-inch thickness on floured surface. Cut out dough using bear-shaped cookie cutter. Place 2 inches apart on ungreased cookie sheets. Using straw, make hole in both arms of each bear, about ¼ inch from ends; cut out heart from center of each bear using heart-shaped cookie cutter.

2. Bake 10 to 12 minutes or until edges begin to brown. Remove to wire racks; cool completely.

3. Prepare Cookie Glaze; reserve ⅓ cup. Stir cocoa into remaining glaze. Place cookies on wire racks set over waxed paper-lined baking sheets. Spoon cocoa glaze over cookies.

4. Add 1 to 2 tablespoons powdered sugar to reserved ⅓ cup glaze. Tint with yellow food coloring, if desired. Dab small dots of glaze onto heads for attaching candies for eyes and noses. Spoon remaining thickened glaze into pastry bag fitted with writing tip; use to decorate cookies as desired. Let stand until glaze is set.

5. Using ribbon, tie bears together through holes in arms. Hang on tree or drape over packages.

BUTTER COOKIE DOUGH

¾ cup (1½ sticks) butter, softened
¼ cup granulated sugar
¼ cup packed light brown sugar
1 egg yolk
1¾ cups all-purpose flour
¾ teaspoon baking powder
⅛ teaspoon salt

1. Combine butter, granulated sugar, brown sugar and egg yolk in medium bowl. Add flour, baking powder and salt; mix well.

2. Cover; refrigerate about 4 hours or until firm.

COOKIE GLAZE: Combine 4 cups powdered sugar and 4 tablespoons milk in small bowl. Add 1 to 2 tablespoons more milk as needed to make medium-thick, pourable glaze.

CHOCOLATE-COVERED RAISINS

Makes about 1½ pounds

2 cups (11½ ounces) milk chocolate chips
1 square (1 ounce) unsweetened chocolate, chopped
1 tablespoon shortening
2 cups raisins

1. Line baking sheet with buttered waxed paper; set aside.

2. Melt chips and chopped chocolate with shortening in medium saucepan over low heat, stirring constantly. Stir in raisins.

3. Drop individual raisins or drop in clusters from spoon onto prepared baking sheet. Let stand until firm.

GINGERBREAD HOUSE

Makes 1 gingerbread house

5¼ cups all-purpose flour
1 tablespoon ground ginger
2 teaspoons baking soda
1½ teaspoons allspice
1 teaspoon salt
2 cups packed dark brown sugar
1 cup (2 sticks) plus 2 tablespoons butter or margarine, softened and divided
¾ cup dark corn syrup
2 eggs
Royal Icing (recipe follows)
Assorted gumdrops, hard candies and decors

1. Draw patterns for house on cardboard, using diagrams on page 77 as guides; cut out patterns. Preheat oven to 375°F. Grease large cookie sheet.

2. Combine flour, ginger, baking soda, allspice and salt in medium bowl.

3. Beat brown sugar and 1 cup butter in large bowl with electric mixer at medium speed until light and fluffy. Beat in corn syrup and eggs. Gradually add flour mixture. Beat at low speed until well blended.

4. Roll about one-fourth of dough directly onto prepared cookie sheet to ¼-inch thickness. Lay sheet of waxed paper over dough. Place patterns over waxed paper 2 inches apart. Cut dough around patterns with sharp knife; remove waxed paper. Reserve scraps to reroll with next batch of dough.

5. Bake 15 minutes or until no indentation remains when cookie is touched in center. While cookies are still hot, place cardboard pattern lightly over cookie; trim edges to straighten. Let stand on cookie sheet 5 minutes. Remove cookies to wire racks; cool completely. Repeat with remaining pattern pieces.

6. Prepare Royal Icing. If desired, some icing may be divided into small bowls and tinted with food coloring to use for decorative piping.

7. Cover 12-inch square piece of heavy cardboard with colored paper or aluminum foil to use as base for house.

8. Place icing in small resealable food storage bag. Cut off small corner of bag. Pipe Royal Icing on edges of all pieces including bottom; "glue" house together at seams and onto base.

9. Pipe door and shutters onto front of house. Decorate as desired with icing and candies. If desired, dust house with sifted powdered sugar to resemble snow.

ROYAL ICING

**1 egg white,* at room temperature
2 to 2½ cups sifted powdered sugar
½ teaspoon almond extract**

*Use only grade A clean, uncracked egg.

1. Beat egg white in small bowl with electric mixer at high speed until foamy.

2. Gradually add 2 cups powdered sugar and almond extract. Beat at low speed until moistened. Increase mixer speed to high and beat until icing is stiff, adding additional powdered sugar if needed.

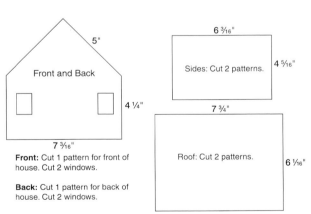

Front and Back

5"

4 ¼"

7 ³/₁₆"

Front: Cut 1 pattern for front of house. Cut 2 windows.

Back: Cut 1 pattern for back of house. Cut 2 windows.

6 ³/₁₆"

Sides: Cut 2 patterns.

4 ⁵/₁₆"

7 ¾"

Roof: Cut 2 patterns.

6 ¹/₁₆"

Sports

OLYMPIC GOLD CAKE

Makes 12 servings

1 package (18¼ ounces) banana cake mix, plus ingredients to prepare mix
1 container (16 ounces) cream cheese frosting
    Blue food coloring
2 cups chopped nuts, toasted*
    Blue, yellow, black, green and red decorating icing
⅔ cup semisweet chocolate, melted

*To toast nuts, spread in a shallow pan. Bake in preheated 350°F oven 5 to 10 minutes or until golden brown, stirring frequently.

1. Preheat oven to 350°F. Grease and flour two 9-inch round cake pans. Prepare cake mix according to package directions.

2. Bake 22 minutes or until toothpick inserted into centers comes out clean. Cool completely before frosting.

3. Blend frosting and food coloring in medium bowl until desired shade of blue is reached. Place one cake layer on serving plate; spread with ½ cup frosting. Top with second cake layer. Frost top and side of cake with remaining frosting. Gently press nuts onto side of cake.

4. Use icing to pipe five Olympic rings using photo as guide. Place melted chocolate in small resealable food storage bag; seal bag. Cut off very small corner from bag; pipe "Olympic Gold" or desired words on cake.

BASEBALL CAPS

Makes about 3 dozen cookies

  1 cup (2 sticks) butter, softened
  7 ounces almond paste
  ¾ cup sugar
  1 egg
  1 teaspoon vanilla
  ¼ teaspoon salt
  3 cups all-purpose flour
    Assorted colored decorating icings
    Colored candies

1. Preheat oven to 350°F. Grease cookie sheets and set aside. Beat butter, almond paste, sugar, egg, vanilla and salt in large bowl with electric mixer at high speed until light and fluffy. Add flour all at once; stir just until blended.

2. Roll one-fourth of dough on lightly floured surface to ⅛-inch thickness. Cut out 1-inch circles. Place cutouts 2 inches apart on prepared cookie sheets.

3. Shape remaining dough into 1-inch balls.* Place one ball on top of dough circle so about ½ inch of circle sticks out to form bill of baseball cap. Repeat with remaining dough balls and circles.

4. Bake 10 to 12 minutes or until lightly browned. If bills brown too quickly, cut small strips of foil and cover with shiny side of foil facing up. Let cool on cookie sheets 2 minutes. Remove to wire racks; cool completely. Decorate with icings and candies as desired.

*Use 1-tablespoon scoop to keep baseball caps uniform in size.

AMERICAN FLAG PIZZAS

Makes 32 servings

2 packages (about 14 ounces each) refrigerated pizza dough
2 cups prepared pizza sauce
1⅓ cups shredded sharp Cheddar cheese
12 cheese sticks or string cheese (about 1 ounce each), quartered
     lengthwise (48 pieces total)
25 pepperoni slices, quartered

1. Preheat oven to 400°F. Lightly coat two nonstick 17×11-inch baking sheets with nonstick cooking spray.

2. Unwrap pizza dough. Roll each one out onto prepared baking sheet. Starting at center, press out dough with hands to edge of pans. Place on center oven rack; bake 8 minutes. Remove crusts, but leave oven on.

3. Spoon 1 cup pizza sauce on each crust. Using back of spoon, spread evenly over crusts. Sprinkle ⅔ cup Cheddar cheese on upper left quarter of each pizza. Arrange 24 cheese strips on each pizza to resemble strips of the flag. Place some strips end to end, if necessary, to make stripes across width of crust. Place 50 pepperoni quarters on Cheddar cheese for stars.

4. Return one pizza to middle rack of oven; bake 8 minutes or until cheese is melted and edges are golden brown. (Do not overbake.) Remove from oven; set aside. Bake second pizza. To serve, slice each flag into 16 pieces when cool enough to handle.

American Flag Pizza

SOCCER BALL

Makes 14 to 16 servings

CAKE & FROSTINGS

4 cups cake batter*
1 cup Base Frosting (page 31)
2½ cups Buttercream Frosting (recipe follows)

DECORATIONS & SUPPLIES

Black licorice strings
Black decorating icing
1 (10-inch) round cake board, covered or large plate

A 2-layer cake recipe or mix will yield about 4 cups cake batter.

1. Preheat oven to 350°F. Grease and flour 2½- to 3-quart ovenproof bowl. Pour cake batter into prepared bowl. Bake 1 hour and 15 minutes or until toothpick inserted into center comes out clean. Cool 15 minutes in bowl. Loosen edge; invert on wire rack and cool completely.

2. Trim flat side of cake. Place on prepared cake board. Trim edges into ball shape.

3. Frost entire cake with Base Frosting to seal in crumbs. Frost again with Buttercream Frosting.

4. Using toothpick, draw pentagon (with five 1½-inch sides) in center of top of cake. Surround pentagon with five hexagons (each with six 1½-inch sides). Repeat pattern alternating pentagons and hexagons to cover entire ball using soccer ball as guide.

5. Cut licorice strings into 1½-inch pieces. Outline shapes with licorice. Fill pentagon shapes with icing.

BUTTERCREAM FROSTING

Makes about 3½ cups

6 cups powdered sugar, sifted and divided
¾ cup (1½ sticks) butter or margarine, softened
¼ cup shortening
6 to 8 tablespoons milk, divided
1 teaspoon vanilla

Beat 3 cups powdered sugar, butter, shortening, 4 tablespoons milk and vanilla in large bowl with electric mixer until smooth. Add remaining powdered sugar; beat until light and fluffy, adding more milk, 1 tablespoon at a time, as needed for good spreading consistency.

FRIED PICKLE SPEARS

Makes 12 servings

3 tablespoons all-purpose flour
1 teaspoon cornstarch
3 eggs
1 cup cornflake crumbs
12 pickle spears, patted dry
½ cup corn oil
   Yellow mustard (optional)

1. Line serving dish with paper towels; set aside. Combine flour and cornstarch in small bowl. Beat eggs in another small bowl; set aside. Place cornflake crumbs in another small bowl.

2. Coat pickle spears in flour mixture, shaking off excess flour. Dip pickle in egg; roll in cornflake crumbs. Repeat with remaining pickles.

3. Heat oil in large nonstick skillet over medium heat. Cook four pickles at a time, 1 to 2 minutes on each side or until golden brown. Remove to prepared serving dish. Repeat with remaining pickles. Serve with mustard, if desired.

BAGEL DOGS WITH SPICY RED SAUCE

Makes 4 servings

1 cup ketchup
1 medium onion, finely chopped
1 clove garlic, minced
¼ cup packed brown sugar
1 tablespoon cider vinegar
2 teaspoons hot pepper sauce
1 teaspoon Worcestershire sauce
1 teaspoon liquid smoke
4 bagel dogs

1. Combine all ingredients except bagel dogs in medium saucepan. Heat mixture over medium-high heat until boiling. Reduce heat; simmer 5 minutes, stirring occasionally.

2. Prepare bagel dogs according to package directions. Serve with sauce.

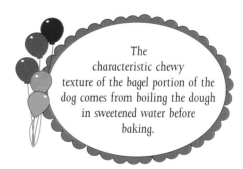

The characteristic chewy texture of the bagel portion of the dog comes from boiling the dough in sweetened water before baking.

Bagel Dogs with Spicy Red Sauce and Fried Pickle Spears (page 85)

FANTASTIC FOOTBALL CAKE

Makes 8 to 10 servings

Chocolate-Covered Coconut (recipe follows)
1 (9-inch) square cake, any flavor
1 container (16 ounces) chocolate frosting
1 cup miniature marshmallows
Red licorice strings
1 (14×10-inch) cake board, covered

1. Prepare Chocolate-Covered Coconut. Cut cake, using photo as guide, into football shape. (Reserve scraps for snacking or discard.)

2. Position cake on prepared cake board. Frost with chocolate frosting and sprinkle evenly with Chocolate-Covered Coconut.

3. Decorate cake using mini marshmallows and licorice strings as shown in photo.

CHOCOLATE-COVERED COCONUT: Line cookie sheet with waxed paper; set aside. Place ¾ cup chocolate chips in large microwavable bowl. Microwave on HIGH 1 to 1½ minutes. Stir after 1 minute and at 30-second intervals after first minute until completely melted. Add 1½ cups flaked coconut, stirring to coat evenly. Spread coconut in single layer on prepared cookie sheet, separating clumps. Refrigerate until chocolate is set. Makes 1½ cups.

BASEBALL SANDWICH

Makes 6 to 8 servings

1 (1-pound) round sourdough or white bread loaf
2 cups mayonnaise, divided
¼ pound thinly sliced roast beef
1 slice (about 1 ounce) provolone or Swiss cheese
3 tablespoons roasted red peppers, well drained
3 tablespoons spicy mustard, divided
¼ pound thinly sliced ham
1 slice (about 1 ounce) Cheddar cheese
3 tablespoons dill pickle slices
2 tablespoons thinly sliced onion
   Red food coloring
   Pastry bag and small writing tip

1. Cut thin slice off top of bread loaf; set aside. With serrated knife, cut around sides of bread, leaving ¼-inch-thick bread shell. Lift out center portion of bread; horizontally cut removed bread round into 3 slices of equal thickness.

2. Spread 1 tablespoon mayonnaise onto bottom of hollowed out loaf; top with layers of roast beef and provolone cheese. Cover with bottom bread slice and red peppers.

3. Spread top of middle bread slice with half of mustard; place over peppers. Top with layers of ham and Cheddar cheese. Spread remaining bread slice with remaining mustard; place over ham and Cheddar cheese. Top with pickles and onion. Replace top of bread loaf.

4. Reserve ⅓ cup mayonnaise; set aside. Frost outside of entire loaf of bread with remaining mayonnaise. Tint reserved ⅓ cup mayonnaise with red food coloring; spoon into pastry bag fitted with writing tip. Pipe red mayonnaise onto bread to resemble stitches on baseball.

STRAWBERRY BLAST

Makes 4 servings

1 box (4-serving size) strawberry gelatin
½ cup boiling water
6 ounces strawberry yogurt
3 cups ice cubes

1. Pour gelatin mix and boiling water into blender; cover, and blend until gelatin dissolves. Add yogurt; cover and blend until mixed. Add ice cubes, 1 cup at a time, covering and blending until smooth after each addition. (After third cup of ice is added, ice may need to be pushed to bottom of blender with long-handled spoon before blending.)

2. Serve immediately or chill 1 hour. When chilled, texture changes to a thicker, soft-gel texture.

CARAMEL POPCORN

Makes 6 servings

1 tablespoon butter
1 cup packed brown sugar
¼ cup water
6 cups air-popped popcorn

1. Melt butter in medium saucepan over medium heat. Add brown sugar and water; stir until sugar is dissolved. Bring to a boil; cover and cook 3 minutes.

2. Uncover pan; continue cooking mixture to soft-crack stage (275°F on candy thermometer). Do not overcook. Pour hot mixture over popcorn; stir with wooden spoon.

3. Spread popcorn in single layer on sheet of foil to cool completely. Break apart.

SLAM DUNK

Makes 12 servings

1 package (18¼ ounces) dark chocolate cake mix, plus ingredients
    to prepare mix
¾ cup crushed chocolate sandwich cookies (about 8 to 10)
1 container (16 ounces) dark chocolate frosting
1 cup prepared vanilla frosting
  Red, yellow and blue food coloring
  Brown mini candy-coated chocolate pieces
  Assorted candy-coated chocolate pieces (optional)

1. Prepare and bake cake mix in two 9-inch round cake pans according to package directions. Cool completely on wire racks.

2. Place one cake layer on serving plate; spread with chocolate frosting. Sprinkle crushed cookie crumbs over frosting. Top with second cake layer. Frost side of cake with chocolate frosting, being careful not to get frosting on top of cake.

3. Blend vanilla frosting and several drops of red, yellow and blue food coloring in small bowl until desired shade of orange is reached. Spread over top of cake. Gently press meat mallet into frosting to create texture of basketball. Arrange mini chocolate pieces on cake as shown in photo. Press chocolate pieces around bottom of cake, if desired.

FIGURE 8 RACE TRACK

Makes 12 servings

1 package (18¼ ounces) chocolate cake mix, plus ingredients
    to prepare mix
1½ cups shredded coconut
    Green food coloring
1 container (16 ounces) chocolate frosting
    White candy-coated licorice bits
    Candy rocks (optional)
    Toy cars and flags (optional)

1. Prepare and bake cake mix according to package directions for two 8- or 9-inch round cakes. Cool completely before frosting.

2. Combine coconut and 4 to 5 drops food coloring in resealable food storage bag; seal bag. Shake bag until coconut is evenly tinted.

3. Place cake layers side by side on large serving platter. Frost tops and sides of layers. Using small bowl or cup as guide, trace 2½-inch circle in center of each cake layer with tip of knife. Sprinkle center of each circle with small amount of coconut. Press remaining coconut onto sides of cake, allowing coconut to come up over cake edges.

4. Use fork to make grooves in frosting. Place licorice bits around centers of cake layers to create lanes. Decorate cake with candy rocks, toy cars and flags, if desired.

Kids' Cake Mix

Contents

Everyday Favorites

CRUNCHY PEACH SNACK CAKE

Makes 9 servings

1 package (9 ounces) yellow cake mix without pudding in the mix
1 container (6 ounces) peach-flavor yogurt
1 egg
¼ cup peach fruit spread
¾ cup square whole grain oat cereal with cinnamon, slightly crushed
  Whipped cream (optional)

1. Place rack in center of oven; preheat oven to 350°F. Lightly grease 8-inch square baking pan.

2. Combine cake mix, yogurt and egg in medium bowl. Beat with electric mixer at low speed about 1 minute or until blended. Increase speed to medium; beat 1 to 2 minutes or until smooth.

3. Spread batter into prepared pan. Drop fruit spread by ½ teaspoonfuls over cake batter. Sprinkle with cereal.

4. Bake 25 minutes or until toothpick inserted into center of cake comes out clean. Cool on wire rack. Serve with whipped cream, if desired.

PEANUT BUTTER & MILK CHOCOLATE CUPCAKES

Makes 24 cupcakes

1 package (18¼ ounces) butter recipe yellow cake mix with pudding in the mix, plus ingredients to prepare mix

½ cup creamy peanut butter

¼ cup (½ stick) butter

2 bars (3½ ounces each) good-quality milk chocolate, broken into small pieces

¼ cup (½ stick) unsalted butter, cut into small chunks

¼ cup heavy cream

Dash salt

Peanut butter chips (optional)

1. Preheat oven to 350°F. Line 24 standard (2½-inch) muffin pan cups with paper liners.

2. Prepare cake mix according to package directions with ½ cup peanut butter and ¼ cup butter (instead of ½ cup butter called for in directions). Fill muffin cups evenly with batter.

3. Bake 24 to 26 minutes or until light golden brown and toothpick inserted into centers comes out clean. Cool cupcakes in pans on wire racks 5 minutes; remove from pans and cool completely on wire racks.

4. Combine chocolate, unsalted butter, cream and salt in small, heavy saucepan. Heat over very low heat, stirring constantly, just until butter and chocolate melt. Mixture should be warm, not hot. Immediately spoon about 1 tablespoon chocolate glaze over each cupcake, spreading to cover top. Sprinkle with peanut butter chips, if desired.

Everyday Favorites

SWEET MYSTERIES

Makes 3 dozen cookies

1 package (18¼ ounces) yellow cake mix with pudding in the mix
½ cup (1 stick) unsalted butter, softened
1 egg yolk
1 cup ground pecans
36 milk chocolate candy kisses
   Powdered sugar

1. Preheat oven to 300°F.

2. Beat half of cake mix and butter in large bowl with electric mixer at high speed until blended. Add egg yolk and remaining cake mix; beat at medium speed just until dough forms. Add pecans; beat just until blended.

3. Shape rounded tablespoon of dough around each candy, making sure candy is completely covered. Place cookies 1 inch apart on ungreased cookie sheets.

4. Bake 20 to 25 minutes or until firm and just beginning to turn golden. Let cookies stand on cookie sheets 10 minutes. Transfer to wire racks set over waxed paper; dust with powdered sugar.

Add to the flavor of these delicious cookies by using white and milk chocolate striped candy kisses instead of the plain milk chocolate candy kisses.

DOUBLE CHOCOLATE CHIP SNACK CAKE

Makes 8 to 10 servings

1 package (18¼ ounces) devil's food cake mix with pudding
   in the mix, divided
2 eggs
½ cup water
¼ cup vegetable oil
½ teaspoon cinnamon
1 cup semisweet chocolate chips, divided
¼ cup packed brown sugar
2 tablespoons butter, melted
¾ cup white chocolate chips

1. Preheat oven to 350°F. Grease 9-inch round cake pan. Reserve ¾ cup cake mix; set aside.

2. Pour remaining cake mix into large bowl. Add eggs, water, oil and cinnamon; beat with electric mixer at medium speed 2 minutes. Remove ½ cup batter; reserve for another use.* Spread remaining batter in prepared pan; sprinkle with ½ cup semisweet chocolate chips.

3. Combine reserved cake mix and brown sugar in medium bowl. Stir in butter and remaining ½ cup semisweet chocolate chips; mix well. Sprinkle mixture over batter in pan.

4. Bake 35 to 40 minutes or until toothpick inserted into center comes out clean and cake springs back when lightly touched.

5. Place white chocolate chips in resealable food storage bag; seal bag. Microwave on HIGH 10 seconds and knead bag gently. Repeat until chips are melted. Cut off ¼ inch from corner of bag with scissors; drizzle chocolate over cake. Cool cake on wire rack before cutting into wedges.

If desired, extra batter can be used for cupcakes: Pour batter into two foil or paper cupcake liners placed on baking sheet; bake at 350°F 20 to 25 minutes or until toothpick inserted into centers comes out clean.

CINNAMON CEREAL CRISPIES

Makes about 5 dozen cookies

½ cup granulated sugar

2 teaspoons ground cinnamon, divided

1 package (18¼ ounces) white or yellow cake mix with pudding in the mix

½ cup water

⅓ cup vegetable oil

1 egg

2 cups crisp rice cereal

1 cup cornflakes

1 cup raisins

1 cup chopped nuts (optional)

1. Preheat oven to 350°F. Lightly spray cookie sheets with nonstick cooking spray. Combine sugar and 1 teaspoon cinnamon in small bowl.

2. Beat cake mix, water, oil, egg and remaining 1 teaspoon cinnamon in large bowl with electric mixer at medium speed 1 minute. Gently stir in rice cereal, cornflakes, raisins and nuts, if desired, until well blended.

3. Drop batter by rounded tablespoonfuls 2 inches apart onto prepared cookie sheets. Sprinkle lightly with one half of cinnamon-sugar mixture.

4. Bake about 15 minutes or until lightly browned. Sprinkle cookies with remaining cinnamon-sugar mixture after baking; transfer to wire racks to cool completely.

SUNSHINE SANDWICHES

Makes 30 cookies

⅓ cup coarse or granulated sugar
¾ cup (1½ sticks) plus 2 tablespoons butter, softened, divided
1 egg
2 tablespoons grated lemon peel
1 package (18¼ ounces) lemon cake mix with pudding in the mix
¼ cup yellow cornmeal
2 cups sifted powdered sugar
2 to 3 tablespoons lemon juice
2 drops yellow food coloring (optional)

1. Preheat oven to 375°F. Place coarse sugar in shallow bowl.

2. Beat ¾ cup butter in large bowl with electric mixer at medium speed until fluffy. Add egg and lemon peel; beat 30 seconds. Add cake mix, one-third at a time, beating at low speed after each addition until combined. Stir in cornmeal. (Dough will be stiff.)

3. Shape dough into 1-inch balls; roll in sugar to coat. Place 2 inches apart on ungreased cookie sheets.

4. Bake 8 to 9 minutes or until bottoms begin to brown. Let cookies stand on cookie sheets 1 minute; transfer to wire racks to cool completely.

5. Meanwhile, beat powdered sugar and remaining 2 tablespoons butter in small bowl with electric mixer at low speed until blended. Gradually add enough lemon juice to reach spreading consistency. Stir in food coloring, if desired.

6. Spread 1 slightly rounded teaspoon of frosting on bottom of one cookie. Top with second cookie, bottom side down. Repeat with remaining cookies and frosting. Store covered at room temperature for up to 24 hours or freeze.

TOPSY-TURVY BANANA CRUNCH CAKE

Makes 9 servings

⅓ cup uncooked old-fashioned oats
3 tablespoons packed brown sugar
1 tablespoon all-purpose flour
¼ teaspoon ground cinnamon
2 tablespoons butter
2 tablespoons chopped pecans
1 package (9 ounces) yellow cake mix without pudding in the mix
½ cup sour cream
½ cup mashed banana (about 1 medium)
1 slightly beaten egg

1. Preheat oven to 350°F. Lightly grease 8-inch square baking pan.

2. Combine oats, brown sugar, flour and cinnamon in small bowl. Cut in butter with pastry blender or 2 knives until crumbly. Stir in pecans.

3. Combine cake mix, sour cream, banana and egg in medium bowl. Beat with electric mixer at low speed about 1 minute or until blended. Increase speed to medium; beat 1 to 2 minutes or until smooth. Spoon half of batter into prepared pan; sprinkle with half of oat topping. Top with remaining batter and topping.

4. Bake 25 to 30 minutes or until toothpick inserted into center comes out clean. Cool completely on wire rack.

MARSHMALLOW FUDGE SUNDAE CUPCAKES

Makes 20 cupcakes

1 package (18¼ ounces) chocolate cake mix, plus
    ingredients to prepare mix
2 packages (4 ounces each) waffle bowls
40 large marshmallows
1 jar (8 ounces) hot fudge topping
1¼ cups whipped topping
¼ cup colored sprinkles
1 jar (10 ounces) maraschino cherries

1. Preheat oven to 350°F. Lightly spray 20 standard (2½-inch) muffin pan cups with nonstick cooking spray.

2. Prepare cake mix according to package directions. Spoon batter into prepared cups, filling two-thirds full. Bake 20 minutes or until toothpick inserted into centers come out clean. Cool in pans on wire racks about 10 minutes.

3. Remove cupcakes from pans and place one cupcake in each waffle bowl. Place waffle bowls on baking sheets. Top each cupcake with 2 marshmallows and return to oven 2 minutes or until marshmallows are slightly softened.

4. Remove lid from fudge topping; heat in microwave on HIGH 10 seconds or until softened. Spoon 2 teaspoons fudge topping over each cupcake. Top with 1 tablespoon whipped topping, sprinkles and cherry.

Maraschino cherries are sweet cherries that are pitted, soaked in sugar syrup, flavored and then dyed a vivid red or green.

Marshmallow Fudge Sundae Cupcakes

OOEY-GOOEY CARAMEL PEANUT BUTTER BARS

Makes 24 bars

1 package (18¼ ounces) yellow cake mix without pudding in the mix
1 cup uncooked quick-cooking oats
⅔ cup creamy peanut butter
1 egg, slightly beaten
2 tablespoons milk
1 package (8 ounces) cream cheese, softened
1 jar (12¼ ounces) caramel ice cream topping
1 cup semisweet chocolate chips

1. Preheat oven to 350°F. Lightly grease 13×9-inch baking pan.

2. Combine cake mix and oats in large bowl. Cut in peanut butter with pastry blender or 2 knives until mixture is crumbly.

3. Blend egg and milk in small bowl. Add to peanut butter mixture; stir just until combined. Reserve 1½ cups mixture. Press remaining peanut butter mixture into prepared pan.

4. Beat cream cheese in small bowl with electric mixer on medium speed until fluffy. Add caramel topping; beat just until combined. Carefully spread over peanut butter layer in pan. Break up reserved peanut butter mixture into small pieces; sprinkle over cream cheese layer. Top with chocolate chips.

5. Bake about 30 minutes or until nearly set in center. Cool completely in pan on wire rack.

BLACK AND WHITE SANDWICH COOKIES

Makes 3 dozen sandwich cookies

1 package (18¼ ounces) chocolate cake mix with pudding in the mix
1½ cups (3 sticks) unsalted butter, softened, divided
2 egg yolks, divided
½ to ¾ cup milk, divided
1 package (18¼ ounces) butter recipe yellow cake mix with pudding in the mix
4 cups powdered sugar
¼ teaspoon salt
2 tablespoons unsweetened cocoa (optional)

1. Preheat oven to 325°F. For chocolate cookies, place half of chocolate cake mix in large bowl. Add ½ cup (1 stick) butter; beat with electric mixer at high speed until well blended. Add 1 egg yolk and remaining cake mix; beat just until dough forms. Beat in 1 to 2 tablespoons milk if dough is too crumbly.

2. Shape dough into 36 balls, using about 1 tablespoon dough for each cookie. Place 2 inches apart on ungreased cookie sheets; flatten slightly. Bake 20 minutes or until cookies are firm. Let cookies stand on cookie sheets 5 minutes; transfer to wire racks to cool completely.

3. For vanilla cookies, place half of yellow cake mix in large bowl. Add ½ cup (1 stick) butter; beat with electric mixer at high speed until well blended. Add remaining egg yolk and cake mix; beat just until dough forms. Beat in 1 to 2 tablespoons milk if dough is too crumbly.

4. Shape dough into 36 balls, using about 1 tablespoon dough for each cookie. Place 2 inches apart on ungreased cookie sheets; flatten slightly. Bake 20 minutes or until cookies are firm. Let cookies stand on cookie sheets 5 minutes; transfer to wire racks to cool completely.

5. Cut remaining ½ cup (1 stick) butter into small pieces. Beat butter, powdered sugar, salt and 6 tablespoons milk in large bowl with electric mixer until light and fluffy. Add additional 2 tablespoons milk if necessary for more spreadable frosting. If desired, divide frosting in half. Add cocoa and 1 tablespoon milk to one half to create chocolate frosting.

6. Spread frosting on flat sides of chocolate cookies, using about 1 tablespoon per cookie. Top with vanilla cookies.

Animal Fun

LADYBUG

Makes 12 servings

1 package (18¼ ounces) white cake mix, plus ingredients to prepare mix
1 container (16 ounces) vanilla frosting
¼ cup red raspberry preserves
   Red decorating sugar
   Candy-coated chocolate pieces
8 dark chocolate discs or mint chocolate cookies
   String licorice and assorted gumdrops
   Large peppermint patty
1 cup flaked coconut tinted green with food coloring

1. Prepare and bake cake mix according to package directions for two 9-inch round cakes. Cool completely before frosting.

2. Place one cake layer on serving plate; spread with frosting. Spread raspberry preserves over frosting to within ½ inch of edge. Top with second cake layer; frost top and side of cake with remaining frosting.

3. Sprinkle top of cake with sugar; decorate with chocolate pieces and discs as shown in photo. Create face with licorice and gumdrops; attach to mint patty with small amounts of frosting. Place patty on cake. Press coconut onto side of cake.

FLUTTER AWAY

Makes 12 servings

1 package (18¼ ounces) white or chocolate cake mix, plus ingredients to
    prepare mix
1 container (16 ounces) vanilla frosting
    Food coloring
1 filled rolled wafer cookie, any flavor
    Gumdrops, gummy hearts and small round candies

1. Preheat oven to 350°F. Grease and flour two 9-inch round cake pans.

2. Prepare cake mix according to package directions. Bake 28 to 31 minutes or
until toothpick inserted into centers comes out clean. Cool completely before
frosting.

3. Blend frosting and food coloring in medium bowl until desired shade is
reached. Cut each cake layer crosswise in half; place two halves on serving
plate, cut sides facing out. Frost top of cake layers; top each half with remaining
halves. Using serrated knife, cut triangles two-thirds down from top of each
half to form butterfly wings as shown in photo.

4. Frost top and sides of cake with remaining frosting. Place wafer cookie
between cake halves to form butterfly body. Decorate wings with candies as
desired.

MISS PINKY THE PIG CUPCAKES

Makes 24 cupcakes

2 jars (10 ounces each) maraschino cherries, well drained
1 package (18¼ ounces) white cake mix without pudding in the mix
1 cup sour cream
½ cup vegetable oil
3 egg whites
¼ cup water
½ teaspoon almond extract
   Red food coloring
1 container (16 ounces) cream cheese frosting
48 small gumdrops
   Mini candy-coated chocolate pieces, mini chocolate chips, white decorating icing and colored sugar

1. Preheat oven to 350°F. Line 24 standard (2½-inch) muffin pan cups with paper liners. Spray 24 mini (1¾-inch) muffin pan cups with nonstick cooking spray. Pat cherries dry with paper towels. Place in food processor; process 4 to 5 seconds or until finely chopped.

2. Beat cake mix, sour cream, oil, egg whites, water and almond extract in large bowl with electric mixer at low speed about 1 minute or until blended. Increase speed to medium; beat 1 to 2 minutes or until smooth. Stir in cherries. Spoon about 2 slightly rounded tablespoons batter into prepared standard muffin cups, filling each about half full. (Cups will be slightly less full than normal.) Spoon remaining batter into mini muffin cups, filling each about one-third full.

3. Bake standard cupcakes 14 to 18 minutes and mini cupcakes 7 to 9 minutes or until toothpick inserted into centers comes out clean. Cool cupcakes in pans on wire racks 5 minutes; remove from pans and cool completely on wire racks.

4. Add food coloring to frosting, a few drops at a time, until desired shade is reached. Frost tops of larger cupcakes with pink frosting. Press top of small cupcake onto one side of each large cupcake top. Frost small cupcakes. Place gumdrops between two layers of waxed paper. Flatten to ⅛-inch thickness with rolling pin; cut out triangles. Arrange gumdrops on cupcakes for ears; complete faces with remaining ingredients.

TEDDY BEAR

Makes 16 servings

1 package (18¼ ounces) chocolate cake mix, plus ingredients to
   prepare mix
1 container (16 ounces) chocolate frosting
4 homemade or store-bought cupcakes
2 heart-shaped gummy candies *or* ¼ cup white chocolate chips
1 package (12 ounces) mini semisweet chocolate chips
2 large white gumdrops
2 small black round gummy candies
¼ cup butterscotch or peanut butter chips
1 red gumdrop or small round gummy candy
   Black and red licorice strings, cut into small pieces

1. Prepare and bake cake mix according to package directions for two 8- or 9-inch round cakes. Cool completely before frosting.

2. Place one cake layer on serving plate; spread with frosting. Top with second cake layer; frost top and side. Stack two cupcakes next to cake to resemble ear and frost; repeat with remaining cupcakes. Place heart-shaped gummy candies in center of ears. Press chocolate chips into side and top edges of cake and cupcakes.

3. Flatten two white gumdrops with rolling pin; arrange on cake to resemble eyes. Use small dab of frosting to attach black candies to white gumdrops. Mound butterscotch chips below eyes to resemble muzzle. Decorate teddy bear face with candy and licorice strips as shown in photo.

Teddy Bear

DOODLE BUG CUPCAKES

Makes 24 cupcakes

    1 package (18¼ ounces) white cake mix without pudding in the mix
    1 cup sour cream
    3 eggs
    ⅓ cup vegetable oil
    ⅓ cup water
    1 teaspoon vanilla
1½ cups prepared cream cheese frosting
    Red, yellow, blue and green food coloring
    Red licorice strings, cut into 2-inch pieces
    Assorted round decorating candies

1. Preheat oven to 350°F. Line 24 standard (2½-inch) muffin pan cups with paper liners.

2. Beat cake mix, sour cream, eggs, oil, water and vanilla in large bowl with electric mixer at low speed about 1 minute or until blended. Increase speed to medium; beat 1 to 2 minutes or until smooth.

3. Fill muffin cups about two-thirds full. Bake about 20 minutes or until toothpick inserted into centers comes out clean. Cool cupcakes in pans on wire racks 5 minutes; remove from pans and cool completely.

4. Divide frosting evenly between 4 small bowls. Add food coloring to each bowl, one drop at a time, to reach desired shades; stir each frosting until well blended. Frost tops of cupcakes.

5. Use toothpick to make three small holes on opposite sides of each cupcake. Insert licorice piece into each hole for legs. Decorate tops of cupcakes with assorted candies.

KITTY KAT

Makes 12 servings

1 package (18¼ ounces) carrot cake mix, plus ingredients to prepare mix
1 container (16 ounces) cream cheese frosting
　Red and yellow food coloring
2 homemade or store-bought cupcakes
¼ cup chocolate sprinkles
　Assorted round and heart-shape candies
　Black licorice string
　Candles

1. Preheat oven to 350°F. Prepare and bake cake mix according to package directions for two 8- or 9-inch round cakes. Cool cakes completely on wire racks.

2. Blend frosting and food coloring in medium bowl until desired shade of orange is reached. Place one cake layer on serving plate; spread with frosting. Top with second cake layer; frost top and side of cake.

3. Cut ⅜ inch from 3 sides of each cupcake to create triangles to resemble ears. Position ears next to cake and frost. Use tines of fork to make frosting resemble fur as shown in photo. Scatter sprinkles around edge of cake and in center of ears.

4. Decorate cat face with assorted candies. Cut licorice strips into 2-inch lengths for mouth. Position candles on cake to resemble whiskers.

Before attempting to remove a cake from its pan, carefully run a table knife or narrow metal spatula around the outside of the cake to loosen.

UNDER THE SEA

Makes 12 servings

1 package (18¼ ounces) chocolate cake mix, plus ingredients
    to prepare mix
1 container (16 ounces) vanilla frosting
    Blue food coloring
    Assorted sea life gummy candies
    Rock candy

1. Preheat oven to 350°F. Grease and flour 13×9-inch cake pan.

2. Prepare cake mix according to package directions. Bake in prepared pan 32 to 35 minutes or until toothpick inserted into center comes out clean. Cool cake in pan about 20 minutes; remove from pan and cool completely.

3. Blend frosting and food coloring in medium bowl until desired shade is reached. Place cake on serving platter; frost top and sides of cake. Decorate cake with gummy candies and rock candy as desired.

BUTTERFLY CUPCAKES

Makes 24 cupcakes

1 package (18¼ ounces) cake mix, any flavor, plus ingredients
    to prepare mix
1 container (16 ounces) white frosting
  Blue and green food coloring
  Assorted candies
  Colored sugar
  Red licorice strings, cut into 4-inch pieces

1. Preheat oven to 350°F. Lightly spray 24 standard (2½-inch) muffin pan cups with nonstick cooking spray.

2. Prepare cake mix according to package directions. Spoon batter into prepared muffin cups, filling two-thirds full.

3. Bake about 20 minutes or until toothpick inserted into centers comes out clean. Cool cupcakes in pans on wire racks about 10 minutes; remove from pans and cool completely.

4. Divide frosting equally between 2 small bowls. Add food coloring to each bowl, one drop at a time, to reach desired shades; stir each frosting until well blended.

5. Cut cupcakes in half. Place cupcake halves together, cut sides out, to resemble butterfly wings. Frost with desired colors; decorate with candies and colored sugar as desired. Snip each end of licorice string pieces to form antennae; place in center of each cupcake.

PUPCAKES

Makes 24 cupcakes

1 package (18¼ ounces) chocolate cake mix, plus ingredients
  to prepare mix
½ cup (1 stick) butter, softened
4 cups powdered sugar
¼ to ½ cup half-and-half or milk
  Red and yellow chewy fruit snacks
  Candy-coated chocolate pieces
  Assorted colored jelly beans

1. Preheat oven to 350°F. Line 24 standard (2½-inch) muffin pan cups with paper liners.

2. Prepare cake mix and bake in prepared pans according to package directions. Cool cupcakes in pans on wire racks 15 minutes; remove from pans and cool completely.

3. Beat butter in large bowl with electric mixer until creamy. Gradually add powdered sugar to form very stiff frosting, scraping down side of bowl occasionally. Gradually add half-and-half until frosting is of desired consistency. Frost tops of cupcakes.

4. Cut out ear and tongue shapes from fruit snacks with scissors; arrange on cupcakes, pressing into frosting. Add chocolate pieces and jelly beans to create eyes and noses.

PONIES IN THE MEADOW

Makes 12 servings

1 package (18¼ ounces) cake mix, any flavor, plus ingredients
    to prepare mix
1 cup flaked coconut
    Green food coloring
1 container (16 ounces) white frosting
    Pretzel sticks
2 small plastic ponies

1. Preheat oven to 350°F. Prepare and bake cake mix according to package directions in two 8-inch square pans. Cool in pans on wire racks 10 minutes; remove from pans and cool completely.

2. Place coconut in small bowl. Add 4 drops food coloring; stir until well blended. Adjust color with additional drops of food coloring, if necessary.

3. Blend frosting and food coloring in medium bowl until desired shade is reached. Place one cake layer on serving plate; spread with ½ cup frosting. Top with second cake layer; frost top and sides of cake with remaining frosting. Scatter coconut over top of cake and around edges of serving plate.

4. Stand pretzel sticks around edges of cake to create fence; arrange ponies as desired.

TIP: Additional decorations can be added to the cake. Arrange candy rocks or brown jelly beans to create a path. Use the star tip on red or yellow decorating icing to create flowers in the meadow.

Holiday Treats

TIME TO PARTY

Makes 12 servings

1 package (18¼ ounces) carrot cake mix with pudding in the mix, plus ingredients to prepare mix
1 container (16 ounces) cream cheese frosting
   Food coloring (optional)
12 chocolate or multi-colored candy discs
   Candy-coated chocolate and peanut pieces
   Tube decorating icing
   Wax letter candles (optional)

1. Prepare cake mix and bake in two 9-inch round cake pans according to package directions. Cool completely before frosting.

2. Blend frosting and food coloring, if desired, in medium bowl until desired shade is reached. Place one cake layer on serving plate; spread with about ½ cup frosting. Top with second cake layer; frost top and side of cake with remaining frosting.

3. Arrange chocolate candies in position of clock numbers on cake. Pipe numbers onto each chocolate candy with icing. Create hands of clock using chocolate and peanut pieces; place on cake at desired time. Press additional chocolate pieces around base of cake as shown in photo. Spell out "Time to Party" on cake with letter candles, if desired.

LUCK O' THE IRISH CUPCAKES

Makes 24 cupcakes

1 package (18¼ ounces) cake mix, any flavor, plus ingredients
    to prepare mix
1 container (16 ounces) white frosting
1 tube (4¼ ounces) green decorating icing with tip
    Green and orange sprinkles, decors and sugars

1. Preheat oven to 350°F. Line 24 (2½-inch) muffin pan cups with decorative paper baking cups. Prepare cake mix according to package directions. Spoon batter into prepared muffin cups, filling two-thirds full.

2. Bake 15 to 20 minutes or until toothpick inserted into centers comes out clean. Cool in pans on wire racks 10 minutes. Remove cupcakes to racks; cool completely.

3. Frost cupcakes. Use icing to pipe Irish words or shamrock designs onto cupcakes. Decorate with sprinkles, decors and sugars as desired.

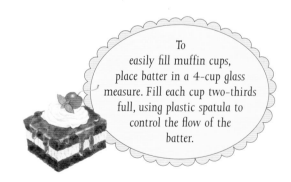

To
*easily fill muffin cups,
place batter in a 4-cup glass
measure. Fill each cup two-thirds
full, using plastic spatula to
control the flow of the
batter.*

FIRECRACKERS FOR THE FOURTH

Makes 30 servings

3 packages (18¼ ounces each) cake mix, any flavor, with pudding in the
    mix, plus ingredients to prepare mixes
3 empty 6-ounce aluminum cans, washed, dried and both ends removed
2 cups strawberry fruit spread
3 containers (16 ounces each) vanilla frosting
    Red and blue paste food coloring
    Black licorice string
1 tube (4¼ ounces) white decorating icing with tips

1. Prepare cake mixes according to package directions. Reserve 1 cup batter.
Divide remaining batter among two 9-inch square baking pans and four 8-inch
square baking pans. Grease and flour cans; cover one end with aluminum foil.
Pour ⅓ cup reserved cake batter into each can; place on baking sheet. Bake
according to package directions. Cool in pans and cans 10 minutes; remove to
wire racks. Cool completely. Wrap in plastic wrap; freeze overnight.

2. Trim two 8-inch cakes to 5-inch squares. Spread one 5-inch cake, one
8-inch cake and one 9-inch cake with ⅓ cup fruit spread each; top each
with remaining same-sized cake.

3. Place 1½ containers of frosting in medium bowl; tint with red food
coloring. Place ½ container of frosting in small bowl; tint with blue food
coloring. Frost sides of 9-inch cake with red frosting; frost top with white
frosting. Frost 1 side of 8-inch cake with blue frosting; frost remaining sides
with white frosting. DO NOT FROST TOP. Frost 1 side of 5-inch cake with blue
frosting; frost remaining sides with red frosting and frost top with white
frosting. Frost can cakes one each with red, white and blue frosting.

4. Place 9-inch cake on serving platter. Top with 8-inch cake, turning at angle
to the right. Frost top right corner of 8-inch cake with blue frosting as shown
in photo. Frost rest of top of middle layer white. Add 5-inch cake as top layer,
also twisting to right at same angle.

5. Add firecrackers to cake top, cutting ends at angles as necessary. Place
remaining frosting in small resealable food storage bags. Cut off tiny corner of
each bag; pipe onto firecrackers as desired. Place small piece of licorice in each
firecracker for fuse. Pipe border around base and top of cake, and up sides with
white decorating icing.

JACK-O'-LANTERN GINGERBREAD

Makes 12 servings

2 packages (14½ ounces each) gingerbread cake mix, plus
    ingredients to prepare mixes
3 teaspoons grated orange peel
  Powdered sugar or frosting
  Gumdrops
  Assorted Halloween cake decorations

1. Prepare cake mixes according to package directions, adding orange peel to batter. Bake in greased 11-inch molded jack-o'-lantern pan about 35 minutes or until toothpick inserted in center comes out clean.

2. Cool 10 minutes on wire rack. Remove cake from pan; cool completely. Decorate as desired with powdered sugar, gumdrops and Halloween decorations.

LIBERTY'S TORCHES

Makes 26 servings

1 package (18¼ ounces) cake mix, any flavor, plus ingredients
    to prepare mix
26 flat-bottomed ice cream cones
1 container (16 ounces) white frosting
    Yellow food coloring
26 red, yellow and orange chewy fruit snacks

1. Preheat oven to 350°F. Stand 24 ice cream cones in 13×9-inch pan and remaining 2 cones in muffin pan cups or in small loaf pan. (Or, place all cones in muffin pan cups.)

2. Prepare cake mix according to package directions. Fill each cone with 2½ tablespoons batter (filling to within about ¼ inch of top of cone base). Bake 30 minutes or until cake tops spring back when lightly touched and toothpick inserted into centers comes out clean. Remove cones to wire rack; cool completely.

3. Stir 4 to 5 drops food coloring into frosting. Frost cupcake tops with frosting. Cut pointy flames from fruit snacks using kitchen shears or sharp knife. Fold or roll flames so they stand upright on their own. Place on cupcakes before frosting sets.

JOLLY OLD SAINT NICK CAKE

Makes 14 to 16 servings

2 packages (18¼ ounces each) yellow cake mix, plus ingredients
    to prepare mixes
3 containers (16 ounces each) vanilla frosting
2 tablespoons milk
  Red food coloring
  Chocolate sprinkles
2 black licorice drops
1 black licorice string
1 round red hard candy
2 dark brown candy-coated chocolate pieces
7 chocolate nonpareil candies

1. Preheat oven to 350°F. Grease and flour one 13×9-inch baking pan and two 8-inch round baking pans. Prepare cake mixes according to package directions. Divide evenly among prepared pans.

2. Bake 35 to 40 minutes or until toothpick inserted into centers comes out clean. Cool in pans on wire racks 10 minutes; remove from pans and cool completely.

3. Using diagrams 1 and 2 as guides, cut out pieces from cakes. Combine one container of frosting and milk. Position pieces on 18-inch square cake board or large tray as shown in diagram 3, connecting with some thinned frosting. Frost entire cake with remaining thinned frosting.

4. Frost face area with some frosting from second container, then tint remaining frosting with food coloring. Frost hat, shirt and pants, reserving small portion of frosting for piping.

5. Pipe design on hat with remaining red frosting using medium star tip. Pipe beard, cuffs and trim of hat with remaining white frosting using medium star tip. Decorate with candies as shown.

BIG CHEEK BUNNY CAKE

Makes 12 servings

1 package (18¼ ounces) cake mix, any flavor, plus ingredients
   to prepare mix
Fluffy White Frosting (recipe follows)
1 (15 × 10-inch) cake board, covered or large tray
2 cups shredded coconut, tinted pink*
2 purchased coconut-covered cupcakes
Red string licorice
Assorted candies

*To tint coconut, dilute a few drops of red food coloring with ½ teaspoon water in a large resealable food storage bag; add coconut. Seal the bag and shake well until evenly coated. If a deeper color is desired, add more diluted food coloring and shake again.

1. Prepare and bake cake mix in two 8- or 9-inch round cake pans according to package directions. Cool in pans on wire racks 10 minutes. Remove from pans to racks; cool completely.

2. Prepare Fluffy White Frosting. Cut out cake pieces from 1 cake round as shown in diagram 1. Position cakes on prepared cake board as shown in diagram 2, connecting pieces with small amount of frosting. Frost cake with remaining frosting; sprinkle with coconut. Decorate with cupcakes, licorice and candies as shown in photo.

FLUFFY WHITE FROSTING: Combine 1 container (16 ounces) vanilla frosting and ¾ cup marshmallow creme in medium bowl; mix well. Makes about 2 cups.

1.

B   1"   B

A

|— 4" —|

2.

B   B

A

BOO HANDS CUPCAKES

Makes 24 cupcakes

1 package (18¼ ounces) cake mix, any flavor, plus ingredients
    to prepare mix
1 container (16 ounces) white frosting
36 large marshmallows
24 black jelly beans, halved
12 orange jelly beans, halved

1. Line 24 standard (2½-inch) muffin pan cups with paper baking cups or spray with nonstick cooking spray. Prepare cake mix according to package directions. Spoon batter evenly into prepared muffin cups. Bake according to package directions. Cool in pans on wire racks 15 minutes. Remove cupcakes from pans; cool completely.

2. Spread small amount of frosting on cupcakes. Cut marshmallows in half crosswise; place one half on each cupcake. Frost cupcakes again, completely covering marshmallow halves.

3. Roll remaining marshmallows between hands until they are about 2½ inches long. Cut in half and arrange on either side of cupcakes to create hands; cover completely with frosting.

4. Create faces using 2 black jelly bean halves for eyes and orange jelly bean half for nose. Swirl frosting on top of ghosts as shown in photo.

Holiday Treats

HEAVENLY ANGEL CAKE

Makes 10 servings

1 package (18¼ ounces) white cake mix, plus ingredients to prepare mix
1 large tray or (17×12-inch) cake board, covered
1 container (16 ounces) vanilla frosting
   Yellow and red food coloring
   White chocolate bar
   Decorations: white chocolate chips; pastel-colored candy-coated
      chocolate pieces; red string licorice; yogurt- or white-chocolate-
      covered mini pretzels; yellow, pink and blue colored sugars

1. Prepare cake mix and bake in two 9-inch round cake pans according to package directions. Cool in pans on wire racks 10 minutes. Remove from pans; cool completely.

2. Using diagrams 1 and 2, cut out cake pieces. Arrange pieces on tray as shown in diagram 3, connecting pieces with small amount of frosting.

3. Tint about half of frosting yellow with few drops of food coloring; tint remaining frosting pink with few drops red food coloring. Frost body and head of angel with pink frosting; frost wings and halo with yellow frosting.

4. Soften bar of white chocolate slightly by holding in hands. Using vegetable peeler, make curls from chocolate bar and sprinkle over body of angel. Decorate with remaining ingredients as shown in photo.

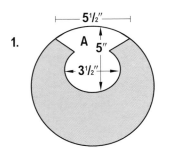

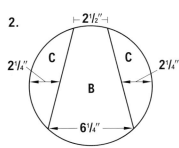

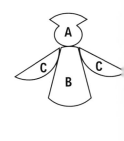

Heavenly Angel Cake

WITCH CAKE

Makes 12 servings

1 package (18¼ ounces) cake mix, any flavor, plus ingredients
    to prepare mix
2 containers (16 ounces each) vanilla frosting
    Green paste food coloring
    Black decorating gel
    Black paste food coloring
    Red licorice strings
1 sugar cone
    Red chewy fruit snack and assorted candies

SUPPLIES
1 (15×10-inch) cake board, covered or large tray
    Pastry bag and medium star tip
1 purchased black party hat

1. Prepare cake mix and bake in 13×9-inch cake pan according to package directions. Cool in pan on wire rack 10 minutes. Remove from pan; cool completely.

2. If cake top is rounded, trim horizontally with long serrated knife. Place cake on prepared cake board. Spread top and sides of cake with 1 container frosting. Transfer about half of remaining container of frosting to small bowl; tint with green food coloring.

3. Using photo as guide, trace outline of witch's head onto frosted cake with toothpick. Fill in face with thin layer of green frosting; outline with decorating gel as shown in photo. Place remaining frosting in another small bowl; tint with black paste food coloring. Spoon into pastry bag fitted with star tip; pipe frosting around edges of cake.

4. Cut hat in half lengthwise. Place one half on cake; discard remaining half. Cut licorice into desired lengths; place around hat to resemble hair as shown in photo. Place sugar cone on cake for nose. Use candies and fruit snack cutouts to make eyes, mouth and eyebrows.

CHILLY SNOWMAN CAKE

Makes 12 servings

1 package (18¼ ounces) yellow cake mix, plus ingredients to prepare mix
1 cup butter brickle bits
22 round peppermint candies
¼ recipe Cookie Glaze (page 75)
   Powdered sugar
4 frosted mini shredded wheat cereal pieces
1 pretzel rod
   Fluffy White Frosting (page 150)
   Coarse sugar (optional)
6 to 8 large marshmallows
   Chewy fruit snack
   Red string licorice
   Assorted candies
1 large tray or (19×13-inch) cake board, covered

1. Preheat oven to 350°F. Grease and flour one 8-inch round baking pan and one 9-inch round baking pan; set aside.

2. Prepare cake mix according to package directions. Stir in butter brickle bits. Divide batter between prepared pans. Bake 30 to 35 minutes or until toothpick inserted into centers comes out clean. Cool in pans on wire racks 10 minutes. Remove from pans; cool completely.

3. Meanwhile, line baking sheet with foil. Arrange peppermints on prepared sheet to resemble hat as shown in photo. Bake at 350°F 4 to 5 minutes or until mints just begin to melt and stick together. Cool completely.

4. Prepare Cookie Glaze. Stir in enough additional powdered sugar to thicken slightly. Using thickened glaze, assemble snowman's broom by "gluing" together shredded wheat pieces and pretzel rod as shown in photo. Let stand until hardened.

5. Arrange cake rounds on tray with smaller round at top. Frost entire cake with Fluffy White Frosting. Sprinkle with coarse sugar, if desired. Place peppermint hat on top of snowman's head. Place 2 marshmallows under hat to support, if necessary. Add broom and decorate rest of snowman as desired.

For the Girls

BALLET SLIPPERS

Makes 12 to 16 servings

1 package (18¼ ounces) white cake mix with pudding in the mix, plus
    ingredients to prepare mix
1 container (16 ounces) vanilla frosting
    Red food coloring
1 tube (4¼ ounces) pink decorating icing
    Pink ribbon

1. Prepare cake mix and bake in 13×9-inch baking pan according to package directions. Cool completely in pan on wire rack. Remove from pan to cookie sheet; freeze overnight.

2. Cut frozen cake in half lengthwise, then cut each half into ballet slipper shape using photo as guide. Arrange slippers on serving platter. (Reserve remaining cake pieces for snacking or discard.)

3. Reserve ⅓ cup frosting. Tint remaining frosting with red food coloring to desired shade of pink. Frost center of each shoe with reserved white frosting, leaving 1 inch on each side and 3 inches at toe.

4. Frost rest of slippers with pink frosting. To add texture, lightly press cheesecloth into frosting and lift off. Outline soles and centers of shoes with pink decorator icing. Tie ribbon into two bows; place on toes of ballet shoes before serving.

SLEEPOVER CAKE

Makes 16 servings

1 package (18¼ ounces) cake mix, any flavor, plus ingredients
    to prepare mix
1 container (16 ounces) white frosting
    Red food coloring
2 individual sponge cakes with cream filling
    Colored sugar sprinkles
4 large marshmallows
    Decorating icing
    Assorted round colored sugar candies
    Red, black or brown licorice strings
4 chocolate peanut butter cups (milk and/or white chocolate)
2 packages (6 feet each) bubble gum tape (pink and/or green)
    Bear-shaped graham crackers

1. Prepare and bake cake mix according to package directions in 13×9-inch pan. Cool cake in pan on wire rack 10 minutes. Remove from pan; cool completely.

2. Blend frosting and food coloring in medium bowl until desired shade of pink is reached. Place cake on serving platter; frost top and sides with pink frosting.

3. Cut sponge cakes in half lengthwise and arrange cakes, cut sides down, on top of frosted cake. Frost sponge cakes; sprinkle with colored sugar sprinkles.

4. Flatten marshmallows by pressing down firmly with palm of hand. Arrange marshmallows at top of snack cakes to resemble pillows. Attach assorted sugar candies and licorice with icing to peanut butter cups to create eyes, lips and hair. Place decorated peanut butter cups on marshmallow pillows.

5. Unwind bubble gum tape; arrange across cake at edge of peanut butter cups to form edge of blanket. Arrange second bubble gum tape around base of cake. Tuck bear-shaped graham crackers around blanket.

GEMS & JEWELS CAKE

Makes 20 to 25 servings

3 packages (18¼ ounces each) lemon cake mix, plus ingredients
   to prepare mixes
3 containers (16 ounces each) white frosting
9 drops lemon extract
   Yellow food coloring
1 package (3.4 ounces) instant lemon pudding
1¾ cups milk
   Assorted candies for decoration

1. Prepare cake mixes according to package directions. Divide batter among 3 cake pans: one 10×2-inch round, one 8×3-inch round and one 6×2-inch round. Bake according to package directions, allowing additional time for larger cakes to bake completely. Cool in pans on wire racks 15 minutes. Remove from pans; cool completely.

2. Combine frosting, lemon extract and food coloring in large bowl; stir until well blended. Prepare pudding mix according to package directions using 1¾ cups milk.

3. Trim tops of 2 largest cakes so tops are flat. Leave smallest cake layer slightly rounded. Cut each cake in half horizontally to make 2 layers. Spread one-third of pudding on bottom half of each cake; replace top cake layers.

4. Place largest filled cake on large serving platter. Frost entire cake. Top with medium cake; frost entire cake. Top with smallest cake; frost entire cake.

5. Decorate entire tiered cake with assorted candies as desired.

TIP: To hold tiers steady, insert a long wooden skewer through center of cake before decorating. Or, place round cake boards between layers. Cut and serve cake one tier at a time.

CORONATION CAKE

Makes 16 servings

2 packages (18¼ ounces each) white cake mix, plus ingredients
    to prepare mixes
2 teaspoons orange extract
2 containers (16 ounces each) vanilla frosting
  Red food coloring
1 to 1½ packages (7 ounces each) flaked coconut
1 costume tiara

1. Preheat oven to 350°F. Line bottoms of two 10-inch round cake pans with parchment paper. Spray pans with nonstick cooking spray.

2. Prepare cake mixes according to package directions, stirring orange extract into batter. Divide batter evenly between prepared pans. Bake 30 minutes or until toothpick inserted into centers comes out clean. Cool cakes completely before frosting.

3. Blend frosting and food coloring in large bowl until desired shade of pink is reached. Place one cake layer on serving plate; spread with frosting. Top with second cake layer; frost top and side of cake.

4. Gently press coconut onto side of cake. Place tiara in center of cake.

Store
leftover shredded coconut
in an airtight container for up to
1 week in the refrigerator or up to
6 months in the freezer.

JOSEPHINE'S TEA CAKES

Makes 10 tea cakes

1 package (18¼ ounces) yellow cake mix with pudding in the mix,
   plus ingredients to prepare mix
2 cups sifted powdered sugar, divided
½ cup (1 stick) butter, melted, divided
8 teaspoons milk, divided
   Sugared Flowers and Fruits (recipe follows)

1. Prepare and bake cake mix according to package directions in 10-inch square pan. Cool completely.

2. Meanwhile, prepare Sugared Flowers and Fruits and set wire rack on large baking sheet.

3. Remove cake from pan and place on cutting board. Cut cake into 1-inch squares and place on wire rack.

4. Combine 1 cup powdered sugar and ¼ cup butter in medium bowl; stir until blended. Add 4 teaspoons milk; stir until smooth. Working quickly, drizzle glaze over half of cake squares, allowing it to drip down sides. Repeat with remaining powdered sugar, butter and milk; drizzle over remaining cake squares. Arrange Sugared Flowers and Fruits on cake squares before serving.

SUGARED FLOWERS AND FRUITS

   Assorted edible flowers
   Assorted small fruits (blueberries, raspberries, currants, kiwi pieces)
1 pasteurized egg white
   Granulated sugar

Brush flower petals and fruit with egg white. Sprinkle generously with sugar; place on wire rack to dry.

BIG PURPLE PURSE

Makes 8 to 10 servings

1 package (18¼ ounces) cake mix, any flavor, plus ingredients
   to prepare mix
1 container (16 ounces) white frosting
  Red and blue food coloring
2 red licorice pull apart twists
1 white chocolate-coated pretzel
  Round sugar-coated colored candies
  Candy lipstick, necklace, chocolate coins and ring (optional)

1. Prepare and bake cake mix according to package directions in two 9-inch round cake pans. Cool in pans on wire racks 10 minutes; remove from pans and cool completely. Reserve one cake layer for another use.

2. Blend frosting, 4 drops red food coloring and 4 drops blue food coloring in medium bowl. Add additional food coloring, one drop at a time, until desired shade of purple is reached.

3. Spread about ½ cup frosting over top of cake layer. Cut cake in half; press frosted sides together to form half circle. Place cake, cut side down, on serving plate.

4. Spread frosting over top and sides of cake. Cut licorice twists in half; press ends into top of cake to form purse handles. Add pretzel for clasp. Gently press round candies into sides of cake. Arrange candy lipstick, necklace, coins and ring around cake, if desired.

FLOWER POWER

Makes 12 servings

**1 package (18¼ ounces) spice cake mix, plus ingredients to prepare mix
Food coloring
1 container (16 ounces) white frosting
5 to 10 large marshmallows
Colored sugar
1 cup multi-colored mini marshmallows**

1. Prepare and bake cake mix according to package directions for two 8- or 9-inch round cakes. Cool in pans on wire racks 10 minutes; remove from pans and cool completely.

2. Blend frosting and food coloring in medium bowl until desired shade is reached. Place one cake layer on serving plate; spread with frosting. Top with second cake layer; frost top and side of cake.

3. Cut each large marshmallow crosswise into 3 slices with clean scissors. Arrange five marshmallow slices in circular pattern on cake to create flower, pressing pieces lightly into frosting. Repeat with remaining marshmallow slices.

4. Sprinkle center of each flower with sugar. Press mini marshmallows into base of cake as shown in photo.

BABY DOLL DRESS CAKE

Makes 1 cake

1 package (18¼ ounces) colorful sprinkle cake mix, plus ingredients to
  prepare mix
1 container (16 ounces) white frosting
  Assorted candies: strawberry licorice string, candy necklace, sour candy
  rounds and wedges, sour candy strips

1. Prepare and bake cake mix according to package directions in 13×9-inch
cake pan. Cool in pan on wire rack 10 minutes; remove cake from pan and cool
completely.

2. Using toothpicks, measure and mark areas to cut (diagram A). At top of
cake, insert toothpicks 1 inch from sides. At 6 inches from top and 2½ inches
from sides, insert 2 more toothpicks. Measure 4 inches from bottom and place
2 toothpicks at sides of cake. Using toothpicks as guides, cut away excess cake.
Larger cake section is body of dress and cut-away sections will become sleeves
and bottom of dress.

3. Place body of cake on serving plate. Position cake sections 4 and 5 for
sleeves. Cut away about 4 inches from narrow end of sections 2 and 3 and
position ends at hem end of dress, trimming to fit (diagram B).

4. Secure sleeves and hem to dress using frosting. Frost top and sides of cake.
Decorate cake with assorted candies to resemble party dress.

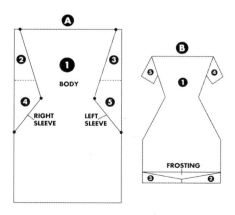

PRINCESS CASTLE

Makes 24 servings

2 packages (18¼ ounces each) cake mix, any flavor, plus ingredients
   to prepare mixes
2 recipes Buttercream Frosting (page 85)
3 sugar ice cream cones
   Blue and red or pink food colorings
4 sugar wafer cookies
2 stick pretzels
4 vanilla wafer cookies, cut in half
   Assorted candies, fruit striped gum and assorted decors

1. Prepare cake mix and bake in four 9-inch square baking pans according to
package directions. Cool in pans on wire racks 15 minutes. Remove from pans;
cool completely. Prepare Buttercream Frosting.

2. Cut 4-inch square out of center of three cake layers. Using cut-out squares
and remaining cake layer, cut 3-inch triangle for door arch. Use 2-inch cookie
or biscuit cutter to cut out 10 circles for towers.

3. Fill and frost first three layers; place on serving plate. If desired, cut out
doorway, as shown in photo, on one side of cake; frost opening. Attach cake
triangle over door with frosting to form arch. Stack cake circles at corners of
castle to form towers. Frost arch and towers. Attach sugar cones on top of
frosted towers as shown in photo.

4. Tint ½ cup frosting blue. Pipe bricks, windows and castle trim. Tint ¼ cup
frosting pink. Pipe accents on door arch and at base of cone towers. Make
drawbridge with sugar wafers and pretzels. Place vanilla wafer halves around
base of castle. Use assorted candies, striped gum and decors to decorate castle
as desired.

For the Boys

JACK IN THE BOX

Makes 8 servings

1 package (18¼ ounces) cake mix, any flavor, plus
    ingredients to prepare mix
1 scoop ice cream or coconut-covered cupcake
    Assorted candies
1 container (16 ounces) white frosting
    Assorted food colorings
    Flat red candy strips or chewy fruit snacks
1 sugar ice cream cone

1. Prepare and bake cake mix according to package directions for two 8- or 9-inch square cakes. Cool completely before frosting.

2. Place ice cream in small dish. Decorate with assorted candies to create face. Place in freezer until ready to serve.

3. Blend frosting and food colorings until desired shades are reached. Cut one cake layer into 4 equal pieces. (Reserve remaining cake layer for snacking or discard.) Place each piece one at a time on serving plate, spreading frosting between each layer. Frost top and sides of entire cake.

4. Press assorted candies around top, base and edges of cake. Create clown collar by pinching candy strips into 4-inch circle; place on center of cake. Decorate ice cream cone, if desired. To serve, place ice cream face on top of candy collar; top with ice cream cone. Serve immediately.

THE SWEET EXPRESS

Makes 12 servings

1 package (18¼ ounces) marble cake mix, plus ingredients
    to prepare mix
1 container (16 ounces) vanilla frosting
    Blue decorating spray
    Decorating icing, any 3 colors
½ cup chopped nuts or crushed cinnamon graham cracker crumbs
7 mini chocolate sandwich cookies
    Sugar-coated sour gummy strips, any colors
    Gummy candy rings
    Assorted small candies

1. Prepare and bake cake mix in 13×9-inch cake pan according to package directions. Cool cake in pan about 20 minutes; remove from pan and cool completely.

2. Place cake on serving platter; frost top and sides with frosting. Spray top third of cake with blue decorating spray to resemble clouds. Draw outline for train cars, using toothpick. Following outline, frost each train car with desired icing color. Sprinkle chopped nuts under train cars. Place sandwich cookies on train cars to resemble wheels.

3. Cut shapes from gummy strips to resemble car connectors, windows, cowcatcher and smoke stack; arrange on train as shown in photo. Arrange gummy candy rings to resemble smoke rings. Decorate train cars and edge of cake with assorted candies as desired.

BUCKET OF SAND CAKE

Makes 10 servings

1 package (18¼ ounces) banana or butter pecan cake mix, plus
ingredients to prepare mix

½ teaspoon ground cinnamon

¼ teaspoon ground nutmeg

1 package (6-serving size) instant butterscotch-flavor pudding mix,
plus ingredients to prepare mix

Clean plastic beach pail and shovel

1½ cups graham cracker or shortbread cookie crumbs, divided

Gummy fish and octopus, starfish and seashell candies, green string
candy and mini chocolate chips

1. Preheat oven to 350°F. Prepare and bake cake mix according to package
directions in two 9-inch round cake pans, stirring cinnamon and nutmeg into
batter. Cool in pans on wire racks 10 minutes; remove from pans and cool
completely.

2. Meanwhile, prepare pudding mix according to package directions.

3. Cut 1 cake layer into 1-inch slices; arrange about one-third of slices in
bottom of pail. Spoon one-third of pudding over cake slices; top with one-third
of cake slices. Repeat layers with one-third of pudding and remaining cake
slices. Sprinkle with 1 cup graham cracker crumbs. Place shovel in cake.
Decorate top of cake with gummy fish and other candies as desired.

4. Cut second cake layer in half horizontally. Place one half, cut side up, on
serving plate. Place pail on top of cake layer. Break remaining cake layer into
chunks; arrange around base of pail. Spoon remaining pudding over cake
chunks; sprinkle remaining ½ cup graham cracker crumbs over pudding. Decorate
with candies as desired. To serve, use shovel to spoon cake onto plates.

FUN FORT

Makes 12 servings

1 package (18¼ ounces) devil's food cake mix, plus ingredients
    to prepare mix
1 container (16 ounces) chocolate fudge frosting
6 square chocolate-covered snack cakes
9 cream-filled rolled wafer cookies
1 tube (4¼ ounces) chocolate decorating icing
1 tube (4¼ ounces) white decorating icing
1 tube (4¼ ounces) green decorating icing with tips
    Sprinkles
    Paper flag and plastic figurines (optional)

1. Prepare and bake cake mix in two 8-inch square baking pans according to package directions. Cool in pans on wire racks 15 minutes. Remove from pans; cool completely.

2. Place 1 cake layer upside down on serving platter; frost top. Place second layer upside down on first cake layer so cake top is completely flat. Frost top and sides. Place one square snack cake in each corner of large cake. Cut remaining two snack cakes in half diagonally; place 1 half cut side down on each snack cake in corners.

3. Attach wafer cookies with chocolate icing to four corners of cake for fence posts, front gate and flagpole. Decorate fort with chocolate, white and green icings and sprinkles as desired. Attach flag to flagpole with chocolate icing and place figurines on top of cake, if desired.

METEORITE MINI CAKES

Makes 12 servings

1 package (18¼ ounces) chocolate cake mix, plus ingredients
    to prepare mix
  Nonstick cooking spray
2 containers (16 ounces each) vanilla frosting, divided
  Assorted food coloring
1 bag (11 ounces) chocolate baking chunks

1. Spray 12 standard (2½-inch) muffin pan cups with nonstick cooking spray. Prepare cake mix according to package directions. Divide batter evenly among muffin cups. Bake 20 to 25 minutes or until toothpick inserted into centers comes out clean. Cool 5 minutes on wire rack; remove from pans and cool completely.

2. Use kitchen shears to trim cupcake edges and form rounded, irregular shapes. Place 2 cups frosting in microwavable bowl and heat on LOW, until melted, about 30 seconds. Tint as desired with food coloring. Stir until smooth. Drizzle frosting over cupcakes, coating completely.

3. Chill cakes 20 minutes. Dot cakes with chocolate baking chunks to make meteorite surface. Melt and tint remaining frosting as desired and coat baking chunks with frosting. Chill until ready to serve.

CUPCAKE CONE ROCKETS

Makes 24 servings

1 package (9 ounces) cake mix, any flavor, plus ingredients
    to prepare mix
24 flat-bottom ice cream cones
24 striped white and milk chocolate candy kisses, unwrapped
    Round gummy candies and sugar candies
18 chocolate wafer cookies

1. Preheat oven to 350°F. Stand cones upright in muffin pan cups. Prepare cake mix according to package directions. Place about 2 tablespoons cake batter in each cone.

2. Bake about 18 minutes or until toothpick inserted into centers comes out clean. Place cones upside-down on wire rack.

3. Place 1 chocolate kiss candy on flat bottom (now top) of each cone, if desired (the warmth of the cones will melt candies slightly and make them stick). Decorate sides of cones by holding sugar candies against warm sides to resemble buttons. Let cones cool completely.

4. Cut each chocolate wafer in half and then into quarters, using sharp serrated knife and sawing motion. Cut three thin slits through thick rim of cone using tip of small sharp knife, spacing slits evenly around cone. Slide chocolate wafer halves into slits to secure.

DUMP TRUCK CAKE

Makes 1 cake

1 package (about 18 ounces) devil's food cake mix, plus ingredients
    to prepare mix
10 chocolate sandwich cookies, broken
    Rectangular cake board
3 containers (16 ounces each) white frosting
    Red and yellow food coloring
    Assorted candy: Blue and red licorice string, round fruit jelly candies,
    rock candy
1 package (4 ounces) miniature chocolate glazed donuts

1. Preheat oven to 350°F. Grease 15×10×1-inch jelly-roll pan. Line with parchment paper; spray with nonstick cooking spray.

2. Prepare cake mix according to package directions. Spread batter evenly into prepared pan; bake 20 minutes or until toothpick inserted into center comes out clean.

3. Meanwhile, place cookies in food processor or blender container; process using on/off pulsing action until cookies resemble coarse crumbs. Set aside.

4. Cool cake completely in pan on wire rack. Lift cake from pan, using parchment paper as aid. Trim ¼ inch off edges of cake using serrated knife. Cut cake into 4 equal sections (diagram A). Wrap each section in plastic wrap; freeze for several hours before frosting.

5. Remove cake layers from freezer; unwrap. Cut rectangular cake board slightly smaller than cake sections. Place small amount of frosting on cake board to secure first cake layer; frost sides and top of cake. Continue stacking and frosting second and third layers. Cut 3 inches off short end of last cake layer; stack on top of other layers so one end of cake has 4 layers and other end has 3 (diagram B).

6. Frost entire cake with more frosting, using up most of second container. Place cake in refrigerator to set.

7. Divide remaining container of frosting into 2 bowls: tint red and yellow using food coloring. Frost hood, roof, lower sides and back of truck with red frosting, avoiding "window" area as shown in photo. Frost rest of cake with yellow frosting. Outline sections with licorice string.

8. Using pastry bag fitted with plain tip (#2 or #3), outline doors and grill with yellow frosting. Attach jelly candy headlights. Carefully lift cake and center on foil. Press 4 donuts into sides of truck to resemble tires. Fill top of dump truck with cookie crumbs and accent with rock candy.

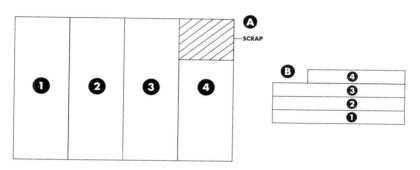

DOLPHIN CAKE

Makes 12 servings

1 package (18¼ ounces) orange-flavored cake mix, plus ingredients
    to prepare mix
1 container (16 ounces) vanilla frosting, divided
  Yellow food coloring
  Blue food coloring
  Mini candy-coated chocolate pieces
  Silver dragées
  Blue sprinkles
  Colored sugar and blue rock candy (optional)

1. Prepare and bake cake mix according to package directions for 13×9-inch cake. Cool cake in pan about 20 minutes; remove from pan and cool completely on wire rack.

2. Reserve ¼ cup frosting in small bowl. Blend remaining frosting and yellow food coloring in medium bowl until desired shade of yellow is reached. Place cake on serving platter; frost top and sides of cake.

3. Draw outline of dolphin in center of cake with toothpick. Blend reserved ¼ cup frosting and blue food coloring in small bowl until desired shade of blue is reached. Spread thin layer of blue frosting within outline of dolphin. Decorate dolphin with chocolate pieces, dragées and sprinkles as desired. Decorate edge and sides of cake with colored sugar and rock candy, if desired.

Super Snacks

CHOO-CHOO TRAIN

Makes 1 (4-car) train cookie

1 package (18 ounces) refrigerated cookie dough, any flavor
All-purpose flour (optional)
Blue Cookie Glaze (recipe follows)
Assorted colored icings, colored candies, small decors and 2 small
   peanut butter sandwich crackers

1. Draw patterns for 4 train cars on cardboard using diagrams below; cut out patterns.

2. Preheat oven to 350°F. Line cookie sheet with parchment paper.

3. Remove dough from wrapper. Roll out dough on lightly floured surface to 18×13-inch rectangle. Sprinkle with flour to minimize sticking, if necessary. Place on prepared cookie sheet.

4. Bake 8 to 10 minutes or until lightly browned. Cool on cookie sheet 5 minutes. Slide cookie and parchment paper onto wire rack; cool 5 minutes.

5. Lay sheet of waxed paper over cookie while still warm. Place patterns over waxed paper. Cut cookie around patterns with sharp knife; remove patterns and waxed paper. Cover with towel; cool completely.

6. Spread Blue Cookie Glaze on train cars as shown in photo. Allow glaze to set about 30 minutes before decorating. Decorate with icings, candies and decors as shown in photo. Use peanut butter sandwich crackers as large train wheels.

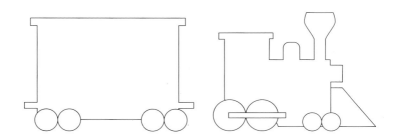

SNAKE CALZONES

Each snake makes 12 to 14 servings

  2 loaves (16 ounces each) frozen white bread dough, thawed
  4 tablespoons mustard, divided
  2 tablespoons sun-dried tomato pesto, divided
  2 teaspoons Italian seasoning, divided
10 ounces thinly sliced ham, divided
10 ounces thinly sliced salami, divided
1½ cups (6 ounces) shredded provolone cheese, divided
1½ cups (6 ounces) shredded mozzarella cheese, divided
  2 egg yolks, divided
  2 teaspoons water, divided
    Red, yellow and green liquid food coloring
    Sliced green olives
    Additional salami or red bell pepper strips

1. Line 2 baking sheets with parchment paper; spray with nonstick cooking spray. Roll out 1 loaf of dough on lightly floured work surface into 24×6-inch rectangle. Spread 2 tablespoons of mustard and 1 tablespoon pesto over dough, leaving 1-inch border, and sprinkle with 1 teaspoon Italian seasoning.

2. Layer half of ham and salami over dough. Sprinkle ¾ cup of each cheese over meats. Brush edges of dough with water. Beginning at long side, tightly roll up dough. Pinch all edges to seal. Transfer roll to prepared cookie sheet, seam side down, and shape into S-shaped snake or coiled snake (leave 1 end unattached to form head on coil). Repeat with remaining ingredients.

3. Combine 1 egg yolk with 1 teaspoon water and red food coloring, and 1 yolk with remaining water and yellow or green food coloring. Paint stripes, dots and zigzags over dough to make snakeskin pattern. Preheat oven to 375°F.

4. Let dough rise, uncovered, in warm place 30 minutes, or 40 minutes if using coil shape. Taper ends of dough to form head. Shape and score tail end to form rattle, if desired.

5. Bake 25 to 30 minutes. Cool slightly. Use olives for eyes and pepper strips for tongues. Slice and serve warm.

5. Add 2 tablespoons flour, 1 tablespoon powdered sugar, lemon peel and ¼ teaspoon yellow food coloring to dough; beat with electric mixer at medium speed until well blended and evenly colored. Shape into 24 balls. Place on prepared cookie sheets. Flatten balls to slightly larger than 1½ inches in diameter. Cut into circles using smooth 1½-inch round cookie cutter. Remove dough scraps; shape into ears. Attach 2 ears to each face. Place 2 candy pieces in center of each ear and place 1 candy piece for nose.

6. Bake 14 minutes or until lightly browned. Cool on cookie sheets 2 to 3 minutes. Remove to wire rack; cool completely.

7. To assemble lions attach faces to manes with icing. Pipe white icing onto faces and press decors into icing for eyes. Pipe chocolate icing onto faces for whiskers.

TIP: Use the remaining half package of refrigerated sugar cookie dough to make lioness cookies! Simply follow the recipe and directions for making the lion faces, but after baking, do not attach them to manes.

LUSCIOUS LIONS

Makes 2 dozen cookies

MANES

   1 package (18 ounces) refrigerated sugar cookie dough
   ¼ cup all-purpose flour
   2 tablespoons powdered sugar
      Grated peel of 1 large orange
   ¼ teaspoon yellow gel food coloring
   ¼ teaspoon red gel food coloring

LION FACES

   ½ (18-ounce) package refrigerated sugar cookie dough
   2 tablespoons all-purpose flour
   1 tablespoon powdered sugar
      Grated peel of 1 lemon
   ¼ teaspoon yellow gel food coloring
      Mini candy-coated chocolate pieces
      Prepared white icing and assorted decors
      Prepared chocolate icing or melted chocolate

1. Generously grease 2 cookie sheets. For manes, remove 1 package dough from wrapper; place in large bowl. Let dough stand at room temperature about 15 minutes.

2. Add ¼ cup flour, 2 tablespoons powdered sugar, orange peel, ¼ teaspoon yellow food coloring and red food coloring to dough; beat at medium speed of electric mixer until well blended and evenly colored. Shape into 24 large balls. Place 12 balls on each cookie sheet. Flatten balls into circles about 2¾ inches in diameter. Cut each circle with fluted 2½-inch round cookie cutter. Remove and discard scraps. Refrigerate 30 minutes.

3. Preheat oven to 350°F. Bake 12 to 14 minutes or until lightly browned. Remove from oven. Cool on cookie sheets 2 to 3 minutes. Remove to wire racks; cool completely.

4. For faces, remove half package of dough from wrapper; place in medium bowl. Let dough stand at room temperature about 15 minutes.

HONEY CRUNCH POPCORN

Makes 12 servings

3 quarts (12 cups) hot air-popped popcorn
½ cup chopped pecans
½ cup packed brown sugar
½ cup honey

1. Preheat oven to 300°F. Spray large nonstick baking sheet with nonstick cooking spray.

2. Combine popcorn and pecans in large bowl; mix lightly. Set aside.

3. Combine brown sugar and honey in small saucepan. Cook over medium heat just until brown sugar is dissolved and mixture comes to a boil, stirring occasionally. Pour over popcorn mixture; toss lightly to coat evenly. Transfer to prepared baking sheet.

4. Bake 30 minutes, stirring after 15 minutes. Spray large sheet of waxed paper with nonstick cooking spray. Transfer popcorn to prepared waxed paper to cool. Store in airtight containers.

VARIATION: Add 1 cup chopped, mixed dried fruit immediately after removing popcorn from oven.

CHOCOLATE BEARS
Makes 16 (4-inch) cookies

1 recipe Chocolate Cookie dough (page 28)
White and colored frostings
Decorating gels
Coarse sugars
Assorted small candies

1. Prepare Chocolate Cookie Dough.

2. Preheat oven to 325°F. Grease cookie sheets. Divide dough in half. Refrigerate one half of dough.

3. Divide remaining dough into 8 equal balls. Cut 1 ball in half; roll 1 half into ball for body. Cut other half into 2 equal pieces; roll 1 piece into 4 small balls for paws.

4. Divide second piece into thirds. Roll two-thirds of dough into ball for head. Divide remaining one-third of dough in half; roll into 2 small balls for ears.

5. Assemble balls to form bear shape on prepared cookie sheet. Repeat with remaining dough.

6. Bake 13 to 15 minutes or until set. Cool completely on cookie sheets. Decorate with frostings, gels, sugars and candies as desired.

To get bright colors and to keep the frostings at the proper consistency, tint them with paste food colors.

Chocolate Bears

about 2"

about 2-1/4"

Diagram 1

Diagram 2

ZEBRAS

Makes about 3 dozen cookies

2 packages (18 ounces each) refrigerated sugar cookie dough
½ cup all-purpose flour
½ cup unsweetened Dutch process cocoa powder*
   Prepared dark chocolate frosting
   Chocolate sprinkles
   Mini chocolate chips and regular chocolate chips

*Dutch process or European-style cocoa gives the cookies an intense chocolate flavor and a dark, rich color. Other unsweetened cocoas can be substituted, but the flavor may be milder and the color lighter.

1. Let both packages of dough stand at room temperature about 15 minutes.

2. Combine 1 package of dough and flour in large bowl; beat until well blended. Combine remaining package of dough and cocoa in another large bowl; beat until well blended. Wrap doughs separately in plastic wrap; freeze 15 minutes.

3. Roll out each flavor of dough separately into 9-inch square between lightly floured pieces of waxed paper. Remove waxed paper. Place cocoa dough on top of plain dough. Cut into four 4½-inch squares. Layer squares on top of each other, alternating cocoa and plain doughs, to make 1 stack. Wrap in plastic wrap; refrigerate at least 4 hours or up to 2 days.

4. Preheat oven to 350°F. Lightly grease cookie sheets. Trim edges of dough square if necessary. Cut dough into ¼-inch striped slices, wiping off knife after each cut; cut slices in half into 2¼×2-inch rectangles. Place rectangles 2 inches apart on prepared cookie sheets.

5. Work with stripes vertically. For each zebra, cut small triangle from top left corner and narrow triangle from top right edge (diagram 1); discard. Cut small triangle from center of bottom edge; place at top of cookie for ear (diagram 2).

6. Bake 10 minutes or until edges are light brown. Cool cookies on cookie sheets 5 minutes; remove to wire racks to cool completely.

7. For manes, spread frosting on cookie edges at both sides of ears; top with sprinkles. Attach 1 mini chocolate chip for eye and 1 regular chocolate chip for nostril on each cookie with frosting as shown in photo.

Zebras

AT THE
ZOO

FROZEN FLORIDA MONKEY MALTS

Makes 2 servings

2 bananas, peeled
1 cup milk
5 tablespoons frozen orange juice concentrate
3 tablespoons malted milk powder

1. Wrap bananas in plastic wrap; freeze.

2. Break bananas into pieces; place in blender with milk, orange juice concentrate and malted milk powder. Blend until smooth; pour into glasses to serve.

Prep Time: 5 minutes

TABLE OF CONTENTS

BLUE COOKIE GLAZE

Makes 1 cup

2 cups powdered sugar
7 to 9 tablespoons heavy cream, divided
   Blue food coloring

Combine powdered sugar and 6 tablespoons cream in medium bowl; whisk until smooth. Add enough remaining cream, 1 tablespoon at a time, to make a medium-thick pourable glaze. Tint glaze with food coloring, a few drops at a time, until desired shade is reached.

JIGGLY BANANA SPLIT

Makes 1 serving

3 **gelatin snack cups (3 ounces each), any flavors**
1 **banana**
3 **tablespoons whipped topping**
   Colored sprinkles
1 **maraschino cherry**

1. Unmold snack cups by dipping partially in warm water for a few seconds. Slide gelatin from cups into center of serving dish.

2. Peel banana and cut in half lengthwise. Place banana slices on each side of gelatin in serving dish.

3. Top with dollops of whipped topping, sprinkles and cherry.

Prep Time: 5 minutes

MOLDED ICE CREAM CONE LOLLIPOPS

Makes about 2 dozen candies

1 package (14 ounces) vanilla confectionery coating pieces*
Orange and/or red paste food coloring for candy
Lollipop sticks
Ice cream cone plastic candy molds for lollipops**
Colored nonpareils

*If coating is bought in block form, coarsely chop before melting.

**For two-toned candies, choose molds with separate ice cream sections.

1. Melt confectionery coating in top of double boiler over hot, not boiling, water. Uncover; stir until coating is melted. Remove from heat.

2. Place half of melted coating in small bowl. For orange sherbet lollipops, stir in orange food coloring, a few drops at a time, until desired shade is reached. Or, for strawberry ice cream lollipops, stir in red food coloring, a few drops at a time, until desired shade is reached.

3. Place lollipop sticks in molds. Stir remaining vanilla coating; spoon into cone portions of molds with small spoon, covering lollipop sticks.*** Refrigerate about 15 minutes or until set.

4. Spoon colored coating into ice cream portions of molds with small clean spoon. (If coating has hardened, remelt by placing bowl over hot, not boiling, water. Stir until melted.) Tap molds on countertop to remove air bubbles. Refrigerate until firm. Set aside any remaining colored coating.

5. Bring candy to room temperature before unmolding to avoid cracking molds. To unmold candy, invert mold and press gently. (If candy does not come out easily, candy is not firm enough; refrigerate 10 minutes.)

6. Drizzle reserved colored coating on cone tops with spoon or small, clean craft paintbrush; immediately sprinkle with nonpareils. Repeat with remaining cone tops. Let stand until set. Wrap in plastic wrap and tie with colored ribbon, if desired. Store in airtight container at room temperature.

***Small metal baby spoons are ideal for spooning melted confectionery coating into intricate sections of candy molds.

MOLDED CHOCOLATE ICE CREAM CONE LOLLIPOPS: Melt vanilla coating as directed and pour all of coating into cone portions of molds. While coating is setting, melt 1 package (14 ounces) dark chocolate confectionery coating. Fill ice cream portions with chocolate coating, reserving some for drizzling. Unmold and drizzle cones as directed in steps 5 and 6. Makes about 4 dozen candies.

NOTES: Confectionery coating comes in a wide variety of colors and flavors. Choose any desired plastic molds and coatings to create your own candies. If you decide to color the coating yourself, paste food coloring for candy works best for vibrant colors without adding liquid to the coating.

OUT OF THIS WORLD

CHERRY TOMATO PLANETS

Makes about 20 appetizers

1 bag (20 ounces) vine ripened cherry tomatoes
¼ cup (1 ounce) shredded mozzarella cheese
20 slices pepperoni

1. Preheat broiler. Slice upper ⅛ inch off stem end of tomatoes using paring knife, keeping tops and bottom pieces next to each other. Seed and core tomatoes using small melon baller or by carefully pinching out core using thumb and index finger.

2. Fill each tomato with cheese; top with slice of pepperoni and cover with tomato top. Secure with toothpick.

3. Place filled tomatoes on baking sheet and broil on top oven rack, about 6 inches from heat source, 3 minutes, until cheese is melted and tomatoes just begin to shrivel.

4. Transfer tomatoes to paper towel-lined plate to drain. Remove toothpicks before serving; serve warm.

MOON ROCKS

Makes 3 dozen cookies

1 package (18 ounces) refrigerated sugar cookie dough
1 cup uncooked quick-cooking oats
¾ cup butterscotch chips
¾ cup yogurt-covered raisins

1. Preheat oven to 350°F. Lightly grease cookie sheets. Let dough stand at room temperature about 15 minutes.

2. Combine dough, oats, butterscotch chips and raisins in large bowl; beat with electric mixer on medium speed until well blended. Drop dough by rounded teaspoonfuls 2 inches apart onto prepared cookie sheets.

3. Bake 9 to 11 minutes or until set. Cool on cookie sheets 1 minute. Remove to wire racks; cool completely.

Quick-cooking oats and old fashioned oats are essentially the same. The quick-cooking oats simply cook faster because they have been rolled into thinner flakes.

PHASES-OF-THE-MOON TOASTED CHEESE

Makes 36 servings
(Makes 18 sets of 8 phases of the moon)

36 slices white bread (about 2 loaves)
36 slices white American cheese
18 slices yellow American cheese

1. Remove top oven rack. Preheat broiler. Line oven rack with foil. Place bread slices in single layer on prepared rack. Replace rack; broil 1 minute or until bread is toasted; flip and broil about 20 seconds more. Remove and repeat with remaining bread slices. *Reduce oven temperature to 225°F.*

2. Top each toast slice with 1 slice white cheese. Cut 4 rounds out of each cheese-covered toast with 1½-inch round cookie cutter; discard scraps.

3. Cut 4 rounds out of each slice of yellow cheese using same cookie cutter. Cut rounds into shapes to resemble eight phases of moon (crescents, halves, three-quarters and full moon). Place shapes on top of toasted white cheese rounds. (Leave some plain to represent new moon.)

4. Place rounds on baking sheet; bake 10 minutes or just until cheese is melted.

CRUNCHY COMETS

Makes 12 to 14 servings

1 package (8 ounces) cream cheese, softened
⅓ cup granulated sugar
1 egg yolk
1 tablespoon all-purpose flour
½ teaspoon almond extract
1 teaspoon vanilla extract
1 package (16 ounces) phyllo dough, thawed
1 cup (2 sticks) butter, melted and cooled
1 can (21 ounces) cherry pie filling
   Powdered sugar
   Colored sugar

1. Preheat oven to 375°F. Whisk cream cheese, sugar, egg yolk, flour, almond and vanilla extracts in medium bowl until smooth. Chill filling 10 to 15 minutes.

2. Unroll thawed phyllo dough on sheet of waxed paper. Lift off one sheet onto work surface and cover remaining dough with sheets of waxed paper and clean, damp towel to keep moist. Brush single sheet of phyllo with thin layer of melted butter. Fold buttered dough in half, brushing edges with additional butter as needed. Dot 1 tablespoon cream cheese filling 3 inches away from corner of rectangle. Top with 1 or 2 cherries from pie filling. Turn exposed corner of dough up over filling and fold in sides to secure. Roll and twist dough into tail shape. Repeat with remaining dough and filling. Reserve extra pie filling.

3. Make 3-inch thick roll of crumpled aluminum foil; place lengthwise on baking sheet. Carefully lay twisted ends of phyllo over foil, bending slightly to form curved comet tails. Brush with melted butter and bake 12 to 15 minutes or until golden brown. Dust with powdered sugar and colored sugar. Serve comets with reserved cherry pie filling on the side.

TIP: Comets may be baked ahead of time and chilled without decorations. Warm in oven to restore crispness before sprinkling with colored sugar.

GALAXY GEL

Makes 16 servings

4 packages (3 ounces each) gelatin (yellow, orange, red and blue)
4 cups boiling water
4 cups ice cold water
¼ cantaloupe, seeded
¼ seedless watermelon
2 large apples, peeled

1. Pour each flavor of gelatin into separate medium bowl. Add 1 cup boiling water to each. Stir 2 minutes to dissolve completely. Add 1 cup cold water to each bowl. Refrigerate 20 to 25 minutes until slightly thickened.

2. Scoop out round planets from cantaloupe and watermelon using both ends of melon ball tool. Cut apples into ⅓-inch thick slices. Use small star cookie cutter or small knife to cut into stars.

3. Spray 2-quart glass bowl with nonstick cooking spray and wipe out lightly with paper towel. Pour thickened yellow gelatin on bottom. Arrange 4 to 5 pieces of fruit on top of gelatin near sides; chill 5 minutes. Carefully pour orange gelatin over yellow gelatin and fruit. Place additional fruit on top of second layer and chill 5 minutes. Repeat with red gelatin and remaining fruit. Finish with blue gelatin; cover and chill in refrigerator 4 hours or more. Unmold onto platter or serve directly from bowl.

Unmold gelatin by pulling it away from bowl edges with moistened fingertips. Dip bowl, almost to rim, in warm water for 10 seconds. Cover bowl with serving plate, invert and shake lose.

SPACE SHUTTLES

Makes 6 servings

6 small bananas
2 packages (12 ounces each) white chocolate chips
3 to 4 tablespoons vegetable shortening
9 mini oval sandwich cookies or vanilla wafers, cut in half
1 bag (6 ounces) black licorice bits
1 bag (14 ounces) red licorice strings, cut into 2-inch pieces
1 tube black decorating gel

1. Peel and trim ends of bananas to make shuttle shapes. Freeze bananas 15 minutes.

2. Melt white chocolate chips and shortening in microwavable bowl. Stir until mixture is smooth and pourable; cool slightly.

3. Remove bananas from freezer. Place 6 forks in 13×9-inch baking pan; arrange bananas on forks in pan, making sure bananas do not touch bottom of pan. Slowly spoon melted white chocolate over bananas, covering completely. Let stand until set. Turn bananas and repeat on other side. Place bananas on parchment-lined baking sheets. Refrigerate coated bananas until white chocolate is firm.

4. Dip cookie slices into melted white chocolate, coating evenly on both sides. Press 3 cookie slices into each shuttle to create flanges at base. Refrigerate until firm.

5. Attach 3 or 4 black licorice bits using melted white chocolate to bottom of each shuttle; insert red licorice strands in center. Decorate with black decorating gel. Refrigerate until ready to serve.

TIP: Make your shuttles soar through the sky! Serve them on blue plates resting on a cloud of flaked coconut.

EARTH'S CORE MEATBALLS

Makes 12 servings

25 medium to large cherry tomatoes, halved and seeded
3 to 4 ounces part-skim mozzarella cheese, cut into ¼- to ½-inch cubes
2 eggs, divided
2 pounds ground beef
1½ cups Italian-style bread crumbs, divided
1 teaspoon salt
¾ teaspoon garlic powder
½ teaspoon black pepper
Cooked pasta (optional)
Prepared pasta sauce (optional)

1. Preheat oven to 350°F. Line two baking sheets with foil and spray generously with nonstick cooking spray; set aside.

2. Insert 1 cheese cube into one tomato half; cover with another half to encase cheese.

3. Lightly beat one egg in large bowl. Add beef, ½ cup bread crumbs, salt, garlic powder and pepper; stir until well mixed. Shape 2 tablespoons beef mixture into rough 2-inch circle. Place cheese-filled tomato in center; bring edges of circle together to completely encase tomato. Lightly roll meatball to form smooth ball. Place on prepared baking sheet. Repeat with remaining meat mixture, tomatoes and cheese.

4. Lightly beat remaining egg in medium shallow bowl. Place 1 cup bread crumbs in another shallow bowl. Dip meatballs one at a time into beaten egg, shake off excess and roll in bread crumbs. Return to baking sheet. Bake 35 minutes until meatballs are slightly crisp and are no longer pink, turning meatballs halfway through baking time. Serve on pasta with sauce, if desired.

SPACE DUST BARS

Makes 1½ dozen bars

1 package (12 ounces) white chocolate chips
⅓ cup butter
2 cups graham cracker crumbs
1 cup chopped pecans
2 cans (12 ounces each) apricot pastry filling
1 cup sweetened flaked coconut
   Additional sweetened flaked coconut (optional)
   Powdered sugar (optional)

1. Preheat oven to 350°F. Grease 13×9-inch baking pan. Combine white chocolate chips and butter in medium saucepan; cook and stir over low heat until melted and smooth. Remove from heat; stir in graham cracker crumbs and pecans. Let cool 5 minutes.

2. Press half of crumb mixture onto bottom of prepared pan. Bake 10 minutes or until golden brown. Remove from oven; spread apricot filling evenly over crust. Combine coconut with remaining crumb mixture; sprinkle evenly over apricot filling.

3. Bake 20 to 25 minutes or until light golden brown. Cool completely in pan on wire rack. Sprinkle with additional coconut or powdered sugar, if desired. Cut into bars.

TIP: For place cards, cut Space Dust Bars into circles and put one at each place setting. In the center of each circle, add a small plastic astronaut figure holding a paper flag with the guest's name on it.

FLYING SAUCER ICE CREAM SANDWICHES

Makes 22 servings

　　3 cups vanilla ice cream
　　1 package (9 ounces) chocolate wafer cookies
　22 mini chocolate-covered peppermint patties
　　Chocolate-covered candies

1. Let ice cream stand at room temperature about 10 minutes to soften slightly. Line baking sheet with waxed paper or foil; place in freezer.

2. Scoop 2 tablespoons ice cream onto one chocolate wafer. Top with second wafer; press wafers together slightly to push ice cream to edges, scraping any excess from edges. Place on prepared baking sheet in freezer. Repeat with remaining ingredients. Leave sandwiches in freezer until frozen solid.

3. Decorate sandwiches one at a time. To attach chocolate peppermint patties to tops of each sandwich, heat table knife over stove burner for a few seconds or until hot. Rub knife on candy until it begins to melt and get sticky. Lightly press candy melted side down to center top of one sandwich. Hold until secure. Reheat knife; melt small area on top of chocolate candy. Stick chocolate-covered candy to melted area and hold until secure. Decorate ice cream edges of sandwich with more chocolate-covered candies. Return to freezer. Repeat with remaining sandwiches.

4. Keep frozen until ready to serve.

CREATURES & CRITTERS

BREAKFAST MICE

Makes 2 servings

2 **hard-cooked eggs, peeled and halved**
2 **teaspoons mayonnaise**
¼ **teaspoon salt**
2 **radishes, thinly sliced and root ends reserved**
8 **raisins or currants**
1 **ounce Cheddar cheese, cubed or shredded**
   Spinach or lettuce leaves (optional)

1. Gently scoop egg yolks into small bowl. Mash yolks, mayonnaise and salt until smooth. Spoon yolk mixture back into egg halves. Place 2 halves, cut side down, on each serving plate.

2. Cut two tiny slits near narrow end of each egg half; position 2 radish slices on each half for ears. Use root end of each radish to form tails. Push raisins into each egg half to form eyes. Place small pile of cheese in front of each mouse. Garnish with spinach leaves.

GRUBS AND BUGS

Makes 28 servings

3 cans (8 ounces each) refrigerated crescent roll dough
2 packages (16 ounces each) cocktail franks (58 franks)
1 bag (about 15 ounces) thin pretzel sticks
  Alfalfa sprouts

1. Preheat oven to 375°F. Grease two baking sheets. Unroll dough; separate along perforated lines into 24 triangles. (Spray hands with nonstick cooking spray as necessary to prevent dough from sticking to them.) Cut one piece of dough with serrated knife into three smaller triangles by cutting through widest corner. Repeat with nine additional pieces of dough. Slice remaining 14 pieces of dough in half.

2. For Grubs, place 1 cocktail frank on longest side of larger triangle; fold sides over ends of franks; roll up to opposite point, pinching dough as necessary to completely cover frank. Place seam side down on prepared baking sheet. Bake 11 to 15 minutes or until deep golden brown. Immediately remove from baking sheet to wire rack; cool completely.

3. For Bugs, place 1 cocktail frank on shortest side of smaller triangle; roll to opposite point. With point facing down, poke 3 pretzel pieces into dough along each side to make legs. Place seam side down on prepared baking sheet. Repeat with remaining smaller triangles and franks. Bake 11 to 15 minutes or until deep golden brown. Immediately remove from baking sheet to wire rack; cool completely. Place bugs on plate of alfalfa sprouts, if desired.

SPECKLED SPIDER COOKIES

Makes 10 sandwich cookies

Chocolate Cookie Dough (page 28)
10 tablespoons raspberry jam or any flavor jam, stirred
1 container (16 ounces) white frosting
Black licorice strings, cut into 1-inch pieces
Chocolate sprinkles
20 cinnamon candies

1. Prepare and chill Chocolate Cookie Dough.

2. Preheat oven to 325°F. Grease cookie sheets.

3. Shape dough into 20 (1-inch) balls; place 3 inches apart onto prepared cookie sheets. Bake 10 to 12 minutes or until set. Remove cookies to wire racks; cool completely.

4. To assemble spiders, place 1 tablespoon raspberry jam onto flat side of 10 cookies. Place flat side of remaining cookies over jam to make body. Spread white icing over top and sides of spider.

5. Insert licorice for legs evenly into one side of spider; repeat on opposite side. Decorate top of spider with chocolate sprinkles and place 2 cinnamon candies on one edge of cookie for eyes.

FISH BAIT WITH GATOR HEADS

Makes 6 servings

6 ounces assorted frozen clam strips, breaded fish pieces or breaded shrimp
3 to 5 drops green food coloring
1 cup tartar sauce
6 (6-inch) bamboo skewers
6 dill pickles
6 to 8 pimiento-stuffed green olives
2 pepperoni pieces, cut into 3 strips each
Mustard

1. Bake seafood pieces according to package directions.

2. Meanwhile, stir food coloring into tartar sauce in small serving bowl until desired shade is reached; set aside.

3. When seafood pieces are cool enough to handle, thread 3 or 4 pieces onto each skewer. Place on serving platter and keep warm.

4. Cut horizontal slit in each pickle for alligator's mouth. Insert strip of pepperoni to make tongue. Slice olives to make eyes and nostrils; attach to pickle with mustard. Arrange alligators around fish skewers and serve with tartar sauce.

BANANA CATERPILLARS

Makes 2 servings

    2 medium bananas
    ¼ cup peanut butter
    4 tablespoons sweetened flaked coconut
    4 raisins
    6 thin pretzel sticks

1. Peel and slice each banana into 10 segments. Assemble caterpillar by spreading segments with peanut butter, pressing segments together.

2. Sprinkle 2 tablespoons coconut over each caterpillar and press lightly with fingertips to coat. Use additional peanut butter to press 2 raisins to one end to form eyes. Break pretzel sticks into small pieces for legs and antennae.

Kids can also be more creative with their caterpillars by adding other types of sliced fruits such as strawberries, apples and/or pears.

NIGHT CRAWLER VEGGIE ROLLS

Makes 18 to 20 pieces

¼ cup sesame oil
1 teaspoon freshly grated ginger
1 teaspoon minced garlic
2 cups snow peas, cut into matchstick-size pieces
2 large carrots, shredded
1 red bell pepper, cut into matchstick-size pieces
1 onion, cut into matchstick-size pieces
2 to 3 cups shredded Napa cabbage
2 cups bean sprouts
1 teaspoon salt
1 teaspoon black pepper
1 package (12 ounces) spring roll wrappers*
  Sweet and sour sauce (optional)
  Peanut sauce (optional)

Rice paper spring roll wrappers can be found in Asian food sections of most supermarkets.

1. Heat oil, ginger and garlic in wok or large skillet over medium heat. Add snow peas, carrots, bell pepper and onion; cook and stir 2 minutes. Add cabbage, bean sprouts, salt and pepper; cook and stir 2 more minutes. Remove from heat and cool.

2. To prepare spring roll wrappers, dip in hot water until soft. Position wrapper with one point facing down. Place approximately 2 tablespoons vegetable mixture in narrow strip across lower half of wrapper. Fold bottom point up and over vegetables and tuck behind filling. Roll packet up once to enclose filling securely. Fold sides in tightly, forming envelope. Finish rolling and brush with additional hot water to seal.

3. Cut tiny eyes and mouths in wrappers and add additional vegetable strips for antennae. Repeat with remaining filling. Cover with plastic wrap and refrigerate. Serve chilled with sweet and sour sauce and peanut sauce, if desired.

POTATO BUGS

Makes about 15 servings

1 package (16 ounces) shredded potato nuggets
6 pieces uncooked spaghetti, broken into thirds
1 carrot, cut into matchstick-size strips
  Sour cream
  Black olive slices
  Ketchup
  Broccoli pieces

1. Preheat oven to 450°F.

2. Lightly grease baking sheets and spread potato nuggets onto sheets. Bake 7 minutes. Loosen nuggets from baking sheets with metal spatula.

3. Thread 3 potato nuggets onto 1 spaghetti piece. Bake 5 minutes.

4. Carefully push carrot strips into sides of nuggets for legs. Attach vegetables with sour cream to create faces as desired.

Potato Bugs and Toasted Cheese
Jack-O'-Lanterns (page 58)

CHEESY SNAILS

Makes 10 servings

1 package (12 ounces) refrigerated French bread dough
5 pieces part-skim mozzarella string cheese
1 egg
1 tablespoon heavy cream
2 tablespoons sesame seeds

1. Preheat oven to 350°F. Line baking sheets with parchment paper.

2. Roll out dough into 12×10-inch rectangle and cut in half to make two 10×6-inch sheets. Cut each sheet into five 6×2-inch rectangles.

3. Slice string cheese in half. Crimp piece of dough around each piece of cheese, leaving ¼ inch of cheese exposed at end. Beginning with other end, roll into coil shape to make snail. Place on prepared baking sheets.

4. Beat egg and cream in small bowl. Brush dough coils with egg mixture and sprinkle with sesame seeds. Bake 20 to 25 minutes or until dough is browned and cheese is melted. Cool slightly before serving.

Cheesy Snails

DRAGON BREATH

Makes 10 servings

2 packages (about 10½ ounces each) refrigerated garlic-flavored
    breadstick dough
  Minced garlic (optional)
1 to 2 tablespoons kosher salt
½ cup mayonnaise
3 tablespoons spicy yellow mustard
1 teaspoon dry mustard
1 teaspoon sugar
1 teaspoon lemon juice

1. Preheat oven to 375°F. Unroll dough onto large ungreased baking sheet.

2. Roll 1 piece of breadstick dough for body of dragon between hands until
dough stretches to approximately 12 inches in length. Place on baking sheet
and twist bottom of dough under to form tail. Make small cut at top and
bottom of stretched dough for mouth and tail using scissors or small knife.
Flatten second piece of breadstick dough slightly and cut in half crosswise to
form 2 rectangles. Make small cut on 1 side of rectangle for wing. Squeeze
edges of uncut side slightly together and press onto right side of dragon body.
Repeat with second triangle and place on left side of body.

3. Sprinkle each dragon with garlic to taste and sprinkle evenly with kosher
salt. Bake 13 to 18 minutes or until golden brown.

4. Meanwhile, blend remaining ingredients in small bowl as spicy serving dip.

NOTE: Dragon Breath can also be made with thawed frozen unbaked dinner
rolls. Use 1 roll for body and another for wings; follow package directions for
rising and baking.

BAT WINGS WITH DRIP SAUCE

Makes 8 servings

  24 **chicken wings (3 to 4 pounds)**
   1 **cup soy sauce**
  ¾ **cup unsulphured molasses**
  ½ **cup beef broth**
  ½ **teaspoon ground ginger**
   1 **cup ketchup**
   2 **tablespoons dark brown sugar**
   2 **tablespoons red wine vinegar**
   1 **tablespoon Dijon mustard**
   1 **tablespoon sesame oil**
   1 **teaspoon hot sauce**

1. Preheat oven to 375°F.

2. Stretch out each chicken wing to resemble bat wing. Arrange wings in single layer, skin side down, in large roasting pan.

3. Combine soy sauce, molasses, broth and ginger in small saucepan; heat over low heat until mixture is smooth and well blended. Pour evenly over wings. Bake wings 30 minutes; turn and bake 30 minutes more or until sauce is thick and sticky.

4. Meanwhile to prepare sauce, combine remaining ingredients in small saucepan. Heat over medium heat until bubbly, stirring occasionally. Let cool slightly before serving.

Bat Wings with Drip Sauce

SAVORY
SELECTIONS

SALMON CELERY TREES

Makes 12 servings

1 can (6 ounces) boneless skinless pink salmon
1 tablespoon minced green onion (optional)
1 tablespoon fresh lemon juice
2 tablespoons minced fresh dill
6 ounces cream cheese
   Salt and black pepper
12 celery stalks
   Fresh dill sprigs, 3 to 4 inches long

1. Combine salmon, onion, if desired, lemon juice and dill in medium bowl until well blended. Add softened cream cheese and mash with fork until mixture is smooth. Season to taste with salt and pepper.

2. Stack celery stalks in pairs. Cut each pair into 3-inch pieces.

3. Spread 2 tablespoons salmon mixture into hollowed section of each celery piece with small spoon or knife. Press dill sprigs into one half of each celery pair before pressing filled sides together. Place upright on serving platter with dill sprigs on top to resemble trees with branches.

"HERE'S LOOKING AT YOU, KID" CHICKEN SALAD

Makes 16 servings

2 large cucumbers (about 12 ounces each)
1 can (5 ounces) chicken breast meat, drained
3 tablespoons mayonnaise
32 black olive slices or about 8 medium pitted olives, sliced (about
1½ ounces total)

1. Peel and cut cucumbers into 16 rounds total (each about 1½ inches thick). Use ½-teaspoon measuring spoon to remove seeds. Hollow out half of cucumber centers to make cups; set aside.

2. Mix chicken and mayonnaise in small bowl until well blended.

3. Stuff each cucumber cup with 1 heaping teaspoon chicken mixture.

4. Cut 16 olive slices into pieces to make face decorations. Top each stuffed cucumber with 2 olive pieces for eyes, ¼ of olive slice for nose and ½ of olive slice for smile.

VARIATION: You can also try this recipe with tuna salad.

Ripe or black olives are green olives that obtain their characteristic black color and flavor from lye-curing and oxygenation. They have a mellow, smooth taste.

PIZZA NACHOS

Makes 4 servings

1 **pound ground beef**
1 **jar (1 pound 10 ounces) RAGÚ® OLD WORLD STYLE® Pasta Sauce**
1 **package (3 ounces) sliced pepperoni (about 1 cup)**
1 **bag (8½ ounces) tortilla chips**
2 **cups shredded mozzarella cheese (about 8 ounces)**
   Your favorite pizza toppings*

Use sliced pitted olives, chopped onions, cooked crumbled sausage, chopped bell peppers or sliced mushrooms.

In 12-inch nonstick skillet, brown ground beef over medium-high heat, stirring occasionally, 5 minutes; drain. Stir in Pasta Sauce and pepperoni and cook 2 minutes or until heated through.

On serving platter, arrange tortilla chips, then top with sauce mixture. Sprinkle with cheese and your favorite pizza toppings.

Prep Time: 5 minutes
Cook Time: 7 minutes

APPLE-CHEDDAR PANINI

Makes 4 sandwiches

1 tablespoon butter
2 cups thinly sliced apples*
¼ teaspoon ground cinnamon
8 teaspoons apple jelly
8 slices egg bread
4 slices (1 ounce each) mild Cheddar cheese

Use sweet apples such as Fuji or Royal Gala.

1. Melt butter in large nonstick skillet. Add apple slices; sprinkle with cinnamon. Cook and stir over medium heat 5 minutes or until golden and tender. Remove from skillet; wipe out skillet with paper towel.

2. Spread 2 teaspoons apple jelly on each of 4 bread slices; top with 1 cheese slice. Arrange one-fourth of apple slices over each cheese slice. Top with remaining 4 bread slices.

3. Heat same skillet over medium heat until hot. Add sandwiches; press down lightly with spatula or weigh down with small plate. Cook sandwiches 4 to 5 minutes per side or until cheese melts and sandwiches are golden brown.

The peak season for domestically grown apples is September through November. Royal Gala apples, which are imported from Australia and New Zealand, are at their peak from April through July.

Apple-Cheddar Panini

HERBIVORE DINO WRAPS

Makes 24 servings

 2 cucumbers
24 large leaves of green leaf or head lettuce (about 3 to 4 heads, depending on size)
 1 container (12 ounces) whipped cream cheese
3½ cups shredded carrots (about 7 medium carrots)
 ½ cup chopped fresh mint leaves
    Salt
 1 cup raisins

1. Trim cucumbers and cut crosswise into 3-inch lengths. Halve each piece lengthwise and slice halves lengthwise into thin strips; set aside.

2. For each wrap, place 1 lettuce leaf on work surface with stem end toward you. Spread about 1 tablespoon cream cheese in lengthwise stripe about 2 inches wide, beginning about 1 inch from top of leaf and ending about 1 inch from bottom.

3. Place 3 to 4 cucumber slices crosswise on cream cheese on lower third of lettuce leaf. Sprinkle with about 2 tablespoons shredded carrots, 1 teaspoon mint and pinch of salt. Sprinkle evenly with raisins.

4. Fold sides of lettuce leaf over filling and roll up from bottom. Place seam-side down on serving plate. Refrigerate until serving time.

SUPER PEANUT BUTTER SANDWICHES

Makes 4 servings

⅔ cup peanut butter
2 tablespoons toasted wheat germ
1 tablespoon honey
8 slices firm-texture whole wheat or multi-grain bread
1 ripe banana, sliced
2 eggs, beaten
⅓ cup orange juice
1 tablespoon grated orange peel
1 tablespoon butter or margarine

1. Combine peanut butter, wheat germ and honey in small bowl. Spread evenly on one side of each bread slice.

2. Place banana slices on top of peanut butter mixture on four slices of bread. Top with remaining bread slices, peanut butter side down. Lightly press together.

3. Combine eggs, orange juice and orange peel in shallow dish. Dip sandwiches in egg mixture, coating both sides.

4. Melt butter in large nonstick skillet. Cook sandwiches over medium heat until golden brown, turning once. Serve immediately.

Prep Time: 15 minutes

Super Peanut Butter Sandwich

FUNNY-FACE CHEESE BALL

Makes 24 servings

2 packages (8 ounces each) cream cheese, softened
2 cups (8 ounces) shredded Mexican cheese blend
1¼ cups shredded carrot, divided
2 tablespoons milk
2 teaspoons chili powder
¼ teaspoon ground cumin
¼ teaspoon garlic powder
2 slices of pimiento-stuffed olive
1 peperoncini pepper
3 pieces red or yellow bell pepper
96 shredded wheat crackers or celery sticks

1. Beat cream cheese, cheese blend, 1 cup shredded carrot, milk, chili powder, cumin and garlic powder in large bowl with electric mixer at medium speed until well blended.

2. Shape mixture into ball. Arrange remaining ¼ cup shredded carrot on top of ball for hair. Use olive for eyes, peperonicini pepper for nose and bell pepper for ears and mouth.

3. Serve immediately or cover and refrigerate until serving time. Serve with crackers or celery sticks.

Prep Time: 15 minutes

SOFT PRETZELS

Makes 18 large pretzels

    1 cup milk
    ⅓ cup butter, softened
    1 teaspoon garlic salt
    3 cups all-purpose flour
    2 tablespoons sugar
    1 teaspoon baking powder
 1½ teaspoons active dry yeast
    2 tablespoons baking soda
      Coarse salt, sesame seeds or poppy seeds for toppings

BREAD MACHINE DIRECTIONS

1. Place all ingredients except baking soda and toppings in bread machine pan in order specified by owner's manual. Program dough cycle setting; press start. Grease baking sheets; set aside.

2. When cycle is complete, remove dough to lightly floured surface. If necessary, knead in additional all-purpose flour to make dough easier to handle. Divide dough into 18 equal pieces. Roll each piece into 22-inch-long rope on lightly oiled surface. Form rope into U shape. About 2 inches from each end, cross dough. Cross second time. Fold loose ends up to rounded part of U; press ends to seal. Turn pretzels over so that ends are on underside. Reshape if necessary. Cover with clean towel; let rest 20 minutes.

3. Preheat oven to 375°F. Fill large Dutch oven three-fourths full with water. Bring to a boil over high heat. Add baking soda. Carefully drop pretzels, 3 at a time, into boiling water for 10 seconds. Remove with slotted spoon. Place on prepared baking sheets. Sprinkle with coarse salt, sesame seeds or poppy seeds. Bake 15 to 20 minutes or until golden brown. Remove from baking sheets; cool on wire racks.

PIZZA SANDWICH

Makes 4 to 6 servings

  1 loaf (12 ounces) focaccia
½ cup prepared pizza sauce
 20 slices pepperoni
  8 slices (1 ounce each) mozzarella cheese
  1 can (2¼ ounces) sliced mushrooms, drained
     Red pepper flakes (optional)
     Olive oil

1. Place focaccia on cutting board; cut in half horizontally. Spread cut sides of both halves with pizza sauce. Layer bottom half with pepperoni, cheese and mushrooms; sprinkle with red pepper flakes, if desired. Close sandwich with top half of bread. Brush outsides of sandwich lightly with olive oil.

2. Heat large nonstick skillet over medium heat until hot. Add sandwich; press down lightly with spatula or weigh down with small plate. Cook sandwich 4 to 5 minutes per side or until cheese melts and sandwich is golden brown. Cut into wedges to serve.

HINT: Focaccia can be found in the bakery section of most supermarkets. It is often available in different flavors, such as tomato, herb, cheese or onion.

Pizza Sandwich

CHEESY POTATO CUPS

Makes 4 servings

4 (6-ounce) baking potatoes, pierced with fork
⅓ cup milk
1 tablespoon butter
¼ teaspoon salt
2 ounces American cheese, cut into 8 cubes
8 fresh broccoli florets

MICROWAVE DIRECTIONS

1. Place potatoes in microwave; cook on HIGH 10 minutes. Slice potatoes in half crosswise. Cut small slice from round ends of each potato slice (this lets them sit upright on plate).

2. Hold potatoes with clean kitchen towel and scoop out centers into medium bowl. Mash potatoes in bowl with fork until fluffy. Add milk, butter, and salt; beat with electric mixer on medium speed until blended. Do not overmix.

3. Divide mixture evenly among 8 potato shells and arrange in microwavable dish. Top each shell with cheese cube and broccoli floret. Place in microwave and cook on HIGH 2 minutes or until cheese melts.

Potatoes have an outer skin, which should be pierced with a fork in several places before being microwaved. This will prevent steam from building up, causing the potato to explode.

SUMMER VACATION

FROZEN PUDDING CUPS

Makes 8 servings

1 package (4-serving size) chocolate instant pudding mix
5 cups cold milk, divided
1 package (4-serving size) vanilla instant pudding mix
   Fresh sliced strawberries

1. Whisk together chocolate pudding mix and 2½ cups milk in medium bowl about 2 minutes. Repeat with vanilla pudding mix and remaining 2½ cups milk in another medium bowl.

2. Divide half of chocolate pudding among 8 plastic cups. Layer half of vanilla pudding over chocolate pudding in cups. Repeat layers; cover with plastic wrap and freeze until firm, about 3 hours. Thaw pudding cups at room temperature 1 hour before serving. Top with sliced strawberries.

Prep Time: 10 minutes
Freeze Time: 3 hours

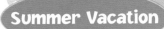
FRENCH FRIED CACTI

Makes 24 servings

    4 cups chicken broth
    2 cups medium-grain rice
1 ½ teaspoons salt
    2 cups grated Parmesan cheese
1 ½ cups (6 ounces) shredded mozzarella cheese
    3 eggs, lightly beaten
       Green gel food coloring
    2 cups panko*
    2 cups vegetable oil for frying

*Panko bread crumbs are light, crispy, Japanese-style bread crumbs. They can be found in the Asian aisle of most supermarkets. Unseasoned dry bread crumbs can be substituted.

1. Combine broth, rice and salt in large saucepan. Bring to a boil; reduce heat to simmer and partially cover. Simmer, stirring occasionally, 15 to 20 minutes or until rice is tender and liquid is absorbed.

2. Remove rice from heat; mix in cheeses until melted. Beat in eggs rapidly. Add food coloring until mixture is pale green. Chill 8 hours or overnight.

3. Line 3 baking sheets with waxed paper. Place bread crumbs on plate. Roll 2 tablespoons rice mixture between hands into 3½-inch log. Roll 2 teaspoons mixture into 2-inch log; attach smaller log to larger log to make branch. Gently dredge rice cactus in crumbs; place on prepared baking sheet. Repeat with remaining rice mixture. Refrigerate about 30 minutes.

4. Line platter with paper towels. Heat vegetable oil to 360°F in medium heavy skillet. Fry 3 or 4 cacti at a time, turning once, about 4 minutes or until golden brown; remove to prepared platter. Sprinkle with salt.

NOTE: Provide a dipping sauce of your choice, such as salsa, warmed marinara sauce or honey mustard.

BANANA SPLIT ICE CREAM SANDWICHES

Makes 9 servings

1 package (18 ounces) refrigerated chocolate chip cookie dough
2 ripe bananas, mashed
½ cup strawberry jam, divided
4 cups strawberry ice cream (or any flavor), softened
  Hot fudge topping (optional)
  Whipped cream (optional)
9 maraschino cherries (optional)

1. Preheat oven to 350°F. Lightly grease 13×9-inch baking pan. Let dough stand at room temperature about 15 minutes.

2. Combine dough and bananas in large bowl; beat until well blended. Spread dough evenly in prepared pan and smooth top. Bake about 22 minutes or until edges are light brown. Cool completely in pan on wire rack.

3. Line 8×8-inch baking pan with aluminum foil or plastic wrap, allowing some to hang over edges of pan. Remove cooled cookie from pan; cut in half crosswise. Place 1 cookie half, top side down, in prepared pan, trimming edges to fit, if necessary. Spread ¼ cup jam evenly over cookie in pan. Spread ice cream evenly over jam. Spread remaining ¼ cup jam over bottom of remaining cookie half; place jam side down on ice cream. Cover tightly with foil or plastic wrap; freeze at least 2 hours or overnight.

4. Cut into bars and top with hot fudge sauce, whipped cream and cherries, if desired.

Banana Split Ice Cream Sandwiches

CONCH SHELLS

Makes 24 servings

2 tablespoons butter, softened
2 tablespoons packed brown sugar
⅛ teaspoon ground cinnamon
1 can (8 ounces) refrigerated crescent roll dough
½ cup raisins
1 egg white, slightly beaten
Granulated sugar

1. Preheat oven to 375°F. Combine butter, brown sugar and cinnamon in small bowl; set aside.

2. Unroll crescent roll dough and separate into pre-scored triangles. Cut each triangle into 3 equal-size triangles. Spread 1 side of each triangle with about ½ teaspoon cinnamon mixture; sprinkle evenly with raisins. Roll each triangle at slight angle from straight-sided base toward triangular tip in shape of conch shell. Place on baking sheet.

3. Brush rolls with egg white and sprinkle with sugar.

4. Bake 8 to 10 minutes or until golden brown. Cool on wire rack.

SERVING SUGGESTION: Design your own sea shore! Make sand by combining equal parts finely crushed graham crackers and raw sugar crystals. Spread sand on a large platter and arrange conch shells on top.

LINCOLN'S LOG CABIN

Makes 12 servings

1½ **cups semisweet chocolate chips**
12 **resealable sandwich bags**
 2 **bags (9 ounces each) thin pretzel sticks**
12 **sheets aluminum foil, each about 12 inches long**

1. Place 2 tablespoons chocolate chips in each sandwich bag; do not seal. Place all bags together on microwaveable plate and heat on MEDIUM (70%) 1½ minutes. Rearrange bags on plate and microwave 1 minute more or until just melted. (Knead bags, if necessary, to allow chips to melt completely.) Squeeze melted chocolate to one corner of each sandwich bag; seal. Snip off very small tip at one corner.

2. Count out 20 unbroken pretzels, 1 bag of melted chocolate and 1 sheet of foil for each cabin.

3. For roof, place 8 pretzels side by side on sheet of foil; squeeze small amount of chocolate between pretzels to hold them together.

4. For walls, squeeze small amount of chocolate about ¼ inch from each end of another pretzel. Lay pretzel across (and perpendicular to) 8 pretzels forming roof, about ¼ inch from end. Repeat with another pretzel at other end of roof base. Squeeze small amounts of chocolate ¼ inch from both ends of these two pretzels; place 2 more pretzels (perpendicular to last 2) in this chocolate. Repeat with 3 more pairs of pretzels (making all 4 walls from 12 pretzels total). Set aside until chocolate cools and sets, about 25 to 30 minutes. To serve, invert so roof is over walls.

NOTE: The chocolate will remain pliable for about an hour after melting. The more chocolate you use as glue, the better the cabins will hold together.

Lincoln's Log Cabin

WACKY WATERMELON

Makes 12 servings

4 cups diced seedless watermelon (1-inch cubes)
¼ cup strawberry fruit spread
2 cups vanilla frozen yogurt
2 tablespoons mini chocolate chips, divided

1. Place 2 cups watermelon and fruit spread in blender. Cover and pulse on low until smooth. Repeat with remaining watermelon. Add yogurt, 1 cup at a time, pulsing until smooth after each addition.

2. Pour mixture into medium loaf pan (8×4 inches) and freeze 2 hours or until mixture begins to harden around edge of pan. Stir well until mixture is smooth and slushy. Evenly stir in 1½ tablespoons chocolate chips. Smooth out top of mixture with back of spoon. Sprinkle evenly with remaining chocolate chips. Cover pan with foil and return to freezer until solid, 6 hours or overnight.

3. To serve, place pan in warm water briefly; invert onto cutting board. Let stand 5 minutes on cutting board to soften slightly. Cut loaf into slices. Serve immediately.

4. Wrap leftover slices individually in plastic wrap and place upright in clean loaf pan. Store in freezer.

Wacky Watermelon

Acknowledgments

The publisher would like to thank the companies and organizations listed below for the use of their recipes and photographs in this publication.

EAGLE BRAND®

The Hershey Company

The Hidden Valley® Food Products Company

Unilever

Index

Index

Index

Index

METRIC CONVERSION CHART

VOLUME MEASUREMENTS (dry)

$1/8$ teaspoon = 0.5 mL
$1/4$ teaspoon = 1 mL
$1/2$ teaspoon = 2 mL
$3/4$ teaspoon = 4 mL
1 teaspoon = 5 mL
1 tablespoon = 15 mL
2 tablespoons = 30 mL
$1/4$ cup = 60 mL
$1/3$ cup = 75 mL
$1/2$ cup = 125 mL
$2/3$ cup = 150 mL
$3/4$ cup = 175 mL
1 cup = 250 mL
2 cups = 1 pint = 500 mL
3 cups = 750 mL
4 cups = 1 quart = 1 L

VOLUME MEASUREMENTS (fluid)

1 fluid ounce (2 tablespoons) = 30 mL
4 fluid ounces ($1/2$ cup) = 125 mL
8 fluid ounces (1 cup) = 250 mL
12 fluid ounces ($1 1/2$ cups) = 375 mL
16 fluid ounces (2 cups) = 500 mL

WEIGHTS (mass)

$1/2$ ounce = 15 g
1 ounce = 30 g
3 ounces = 90 g
4 ounces = 120 g
8 ounces = 225 g
10 ounces = 285 g
12 ounces = 360 g
16 ounces = 1 pound = 450 g

DIMENSIONS

$1/16$ inch = 2 mm
$1/8$ inch = 3 mm
$1/4$ inch = 6 mm
$1/2$ inch = 1.5 cm
$3/4$ inch = 2 cm
1 inch = 2.5 cm

OVEN TEMPERATURES

250°F = 120°C
275°F = 140°C
300°F = 150°C
325°F = 160°C
350°F = 180°C
375°F = 190°C
400°F = 200°C
425°F = 220°C
450°F = 230°C

BAKING PAN SIZES

Utensil	Size in Inches/Quarts	Metric Volume	Size in Centimeters
Baking or Cake Pan (square or rectangular)	$8 \times 8 \times 2$	2 L	$20 \times 20 \times 5$
	$9 \times 9 \times 2$	2.5 L	$23 \times 23 \times 5$
	$12 \times 8 \times 2$	3 L	$30 \times 20 \times 5$
	$13 \times 9 \times 2$	3.5 L	$33 \times 23 \times 5$
Loaf Pan	$8 \times 4 \times 3$	1.5 L	$20 \times 10 \times 7$
	$9 \times 5 \times 3$	2 L	$23 \times 13 \times 7$
Round Layer Cake Pan	$8 \times 1 1/2$	1.2 L	20×4
	$9 \times 1 1/2$	1.5 L	23×4
Pie Plate	$8 \times 1 1/4$	750 mL	20×3
	$9 \times 1 1/4$	1 L	23×3
Baking Dish or Casserole	1 quart	1 L	—
	$1 1/2$ quart	1.5 L	—
	2 quart	2 L	—